ソフトロー・デモクラシーによる法改革

THE REFORM OF JAPANESE LAW VIA SOFT LAW DEMOCRACY

法学博士・弁護士 **遠藤直哉**
Dr. *Naoya Endo*

Art Days

ソフトロー・デモクラシーによる法改革・目次

序章

- I 要旨 9
- II 応答的法としての法システムの4段階ピラミッドモデル 10
- III 法の支配の実質化 12
- IV 規制改革と民事司法の強化 17
- V 村上春樹「1Q84」 18

第1章 理想としての「法システムの4段階ピラミッドモデル」 21

I 応答的法への進展（実質的法の支配） 22
1. 図1 ピラミッドモデル（刑事→民事→行政→自主規律）応答的法型 22
2. 図2 逆ピラミッドモデル（行政→中間団体→刑事→民事）形式法型 22
3. 規制改革 23

II 各段階の役割強化（改革） 26
1. 刑事 26
2. 民事 27
3. 行政（政府、自治体） 27
4. 自主規律（民間） 27

III 具体例 28
1. バブル経済崩壊の責任追及 28
2. 特定秘密保護法 29
3. ハンセン病患者の損害賠償請求訴訟 29
4. 生殖補助医療 30

Ⅳ ソフトロー・デモクラシー 31
1. ハードロー 31
2. ソフトロー 32
3. 代表制デモクラシーの限界 33
4. ソフトローの活用（ボトムアップ） 33
5. ソフトローの特性と効用 34
6. 裁判所の判決 36

第2章 刑事裁判システムの改革 39

Ⅰ 重点化と代替案 40
1. 暴力事犯 40
2. 市場と医療への過剰介入 40
3. ソフトローによる企業犯罪対策 41
4. 給付行政の適正化 43

Ⅱ 刑事実務の後進性（抑圧性）（4つの欠陥の改革） 43
1. 保釈の拡大（人質司法の解消） 43
2. 取調の可視化（自白調書偏重） 44
3. 全面証拠開示の実現 44
4. Beyond a reasonable doubt の採用 45

Ⅲ 欠陥を是正できない理由 45
1. 警察と検察 45
2. 特捜検察 46
3. 学界の意見 46
4. 検察改革 46

Ⅳ　**裁判員裁判**　46
　　　　1．無罪率の上昇　47
　　　　2．被告人の選択権　47
　　　　3．評議の秘密　47

第3章　**民事裁判の改革**　49

　　Ⅰ　**民事裁判の欠陥**　50
　　　　1．被害救済の強化の必要性　50
　　　　2．証拠開示の拡大の必要性　51

　　Ⅱ　**分割責任の拡大の必要性**　52
　　　　1．不法行為法での拡大　52
　　　　2．契約法と信義誠実原則　53

　　Ⅲ　**法政策機能強化の必要性**　53
　　　　1．社会的責任から法的責任へ（米国）　53
　　　　2．行政への不介入（日本）　54

第4章　**行政規制（予防）**　55

　　Ⅰ　**予防的機能**　56
　　　　1．予防的立法　57
　　　　2．ソフトロー　57
　　　　3．予防のための抑止措置　57

　　Ⅱ　**行政ソフトローの大きな展開**　58
　　　　1．外部化現象　58

2. 公表　59

III　行政ソフトローの民主的運用　59
1. 行政手続法　60
2. パブリック・コメント手続き（意見公募手続き）　60
3. 法令適用事前申請確認手続　61

IV　行政ソフトローに対する民事的コントロール　61
1. 無効確認と差止請求（行政の裁量権の限界）　62
2. 国家賠償請求訴訟　63

第5章　自主規律（自己統治）　65

I　民間ソフトローの役割　66
1. 中間団体の新しい役割　66
2. ソフトローの社会適合機能　67
3. 自己統治と自治　68

II　民間ソフトローの法的効力（法的拘束力）　70
1. 民間ソフトローの正当性　70
2. 拘束力の強弱　71
3. 制裁方法（有効なもの）　71
4. 司法審査（無効の場合）　72

III　安全規制と消費者保護　73
1. 規制改革　73
2. 消費者裁判手続特例法　74

第6章　社会国家における財政の課題　75

- I　財政支出　76
  - 1.財政収支　76
  - 2.公共事業費　77
  - 3.社会保障費　77

- II　不正受給対策　78

- III　情報公開制度　79

- IV　医療保険制度　80
  - 1.同一建物居住者対象の報酬減額について　81
  - 2.訪問診療の16km制限について　82

第7章　参政権と政党　85

- I　二大政党から多数政党へ　86

- II　低い選挙率と死票　87

- III　一票の格差（憲法違反）　87

- IV　公務員制度改革　88

第8章　3.11大震災の放射能被害　91

- I　帰宅困難地区　92

目次

Ⅱ 放射能身体許容レベル 92

Ⅲ 原子力発電廃止政策 93

第9章 法の創造と法のイノベーター 95

Ⅰ 司法の劣位 96
1. 2割司法の時代 96
2. 日弁連の改革運動 97

Ⅱ 司法改革 97
1. 司法改革審議会意見書 97
2. 隣接士業の恒久化の危機 98

Ⅲ 法科大学院改革 99
1. 法曹像 99
2. 隣接士業の廃止 99
3. 研修弁護士と法曹一元 100
4. 法科大学院協議会の重大な役割 101

Ⅳ 最高裁判所の司法消極主義 101
1. 違憲立法審査権の不行使 101
2. 最高裁判所裁判官の任命 102

巻末・主要な参考文献 (英文ページ145)

序章

I　要旨

　日本において、法の支配の実質化には、応答的法と司法積極主義への法の創造的改革が必要となる。そのためには、今まで法と言われたきたものをハードローとソフトローに分けて考察することが必要である。特に、ソフトローデモクラシーというべきものが改革の要諦といえる。ソフトロー改革を通じてのハードロー改革への道は、ボトムアップによる法の支配の進展を促す。

　法の運用においては、強制力の強さから順に、刑事司法、民事司法、行政(予防)、民間(自主規律)のピラミッド型をもって法の機能と役割を明確にする。日本では、戦後、自律的法の発展が見られたが、刑事制裁を中心とする抑圧的法への後退、司法消極主義の固定化、部分社会の法理の導入など閉塞的状況が見られる。これに対して新たに、行政と民間団体の自主規律の開放化的強化とソフトローの柔軟化的運用をもって、応答的法への道を探る。

　その結果、法科大学院がこの法の運用の改革教育を担う最も重要な役割をもつことを明らかにする。法のトータルな改革を担う法曹教育を拡充すべきであり、隣接士業の分野の教育（隣接士業の廃止）、司法修習の分野の教育（司法研修所

の廃止・研修弁護士制度・法曹一元）を、完全にカバーし、法社会をリードすべきである。これにより、法の研究者及び教育者が最高レベルの実務により多く参加することが必須であることが明らかとなる。

Ⅱ 応答的法としての法システムの4段階ピラミッドモデル

　日本は第二次大戦からの復興、高度経済成長、バブル経済、人口増加の時代の中で、欧米のモデルを模して、自由民主党の一党支配のトップダウン方式により政策を遂行できた。しかし、1990年代から大きなデフレ経済、経済の低成長、2005年から人口減少の時代となった。経済と文化の面で成熟した先進国家となった。人々の生活と文化は多様化し、グローバリゼーションも急速に進んだ。科学技術はめざましい発展を遂げ、ビジネスや投資は新しい手法を切り開いていった。

　欧米では、先進国への歩みと共に絶え間のない大きな法の革新がなされてきた。しかし、日本では世界の先進国における社会変動の中にいるにも関わらず、法の対応は常に遅れ、法的改革は進まなかった。欧米にみられるボトムアップの法の形成が必要な時代となったが、なしえなかった。市場経済や医療の分野では、社会システムを整備して紛争や犯罪を予防すべきであった。しかし、日本では過去20年間、後進国型の刑事司法の取締りを中心とする古い法規制に依存したま

まで、次々に企業家、官僚、公認会計士、弁護士、医師を刑事処罰してきた。特に逮捕についてテレビや週刊誌が過剰に報道し、劇場型の見世物のようになっていった。ローマのコロッシアムの映像のようである。

私は長い間の実務経験と欧米の法理論の研究により、刑事処罰を中心にしないで、民事裁判を強化し、行政と民間の担う予防を中心とする「法の支配の再構築」をするべきと考えた。当然のことながら、代議制民主主義を前提とするも、世界的にその限界が明らかとなっている状況で、法の運用を担う分野の役割を明確にするために、ピラミッドモデルとして権力（法的拘束力）の強い順に、上から刑事（検察、警察）、民事（弁護士、裁判所）、行政、民間の４段階とし、各役割を強化するべき方向を示すものである。

国際的な視点で考察したことから、本書の構想の骨子を、2011年の国際犯罪学会第１６回世界大会（神戸市）で報告した。本年（2014年）５月に日本法社会学会学術大会、及び米国法社会学会(1)（ミネアポリス）で、７月に国際社会学会（法社会学研究委員会）の世界大会（横浜）で報告する。また、本年10月に国際弁護士協会の世界大会（東京）が開催される。これらの大会での発表を目的に本書を出版した。そして日本の皆様には、本書における応答的法を目指すソフトロー・デモクラシーと４段階ピラミッドモデルを理解頂ければ、皆様

の活動する場所で各人の役割を果たすことにより、大きく法の改革に寄与できることが明らかになるでしょう。

Ⅲ　法の支配の実質化

　1978年、ノネとセルズニックは「法の支配」の歴史的発展を、刑事制裁に依存する「抑圧的法」から、民事法による規律を核とする「自律的法」へ、更に行政と民間との相互協力を強化する「応答的法」への過程を類型化して示した。現代の先進国においては、応答的法を理想とする。欧米では、「応答的法」の社会が発展しているが、日本では、民事司法が充分に機能していないために、「自律的法」への歩みの中で、しばしば「抑圧的法」へ後退する現象が起きている。換言すれば「法の支配」の空洞化である。2011年、タマハナは「法の支配」について、過去の思想をまとめ、議会の制定法であれば悪法でもよいとする「形式的な法の支配」ではなく、憲法の保障する自由や人権、民主主義や福祉国家の価値を実現するための「実質的な法の支配」の実現が重要であるとした。本書では上記概念を用いつつ、現実に機能している法制度を具体的に把握して、これをどのように改革するべきかを示すこととする。

　日本では、江戸時代から、明治、大正を経て第2次世界大戦まで、刑事権力による支配を中心とする「抑圧的法」の国家であった。しかし、第2次世界大戦後は、連合国軍（米

国）の指令により、基本的人権の保障、平和主義、違憲立法審査権などを含む民主憲法の成立により、近代法治国家、「自律的法」の国家へと発展した。しかし、冷戦下での社会主義勢力に対する刑事弾圧は継続し、公害、労災、消費者被害などについての民事救済は進まず、行政上の予防措置もとられなかった。すなわち、議会の制定する法律は次々と制定されていったので、「形式的な法の支配」は継続したと言えるが、生命、身体、生活、権利等を法により現実に保障する「実質的な法の支配」は発展しなかった。それは、基本的人権を公共の福祉の理由をもって制限する悪法や、法の運用における人権制限に対して、裁判所は憲法違反とする決定を出さず、違憲立法審査権を、全くと言っていい程、行使しなかったことからも明らかであった。すなわち、日本社会が急激に経済成長する中で、社会の発展と共に、法そのものが改革されるべきという「応答的法」の段階へ進む事ができなかった。

　多くの深刻な公害、悪質な消費者被害も事後の刑事処罰によった。特に、バブル経済の崩壊による社会の大混乱を治めるため、警察と検察による企業関係者への責任追及が大量に起こった。医療過誤が増加し、患者被害者の民事救済が進まないために、欧米では見られないような、医師及び看護師への刑事制裁などが発生した。つまり、「抑圧的法」社会への後退を示した。他方で、江戸時代から続いてきた全国の多く

の暴力団は、支配層と関係を持ちながら継続していた。いわば、表と裏の暴力の支配が続いた。

このような状況において、「法の支配」を実質化すべきことを主張する研究者、ジャーナリスト、政党、弁護士会が様々な提言をし、応答的法の実現への成果をあげる努力をしてきたが、未だ困難な状況が続いている。つまり、米国、EUに比べ法の改革は著しく遅れている。その最も大きな原因は、日本では、法律家も含めて国民は法を受動的に受け取るのみで、自ら積極的に創造することがないからである。法の支配の法とは、主としてハードロー（議会の法）を対象としている。日本ではほとんどのハードローを、欧米のものを真似して作るので、既に受動的である。研究者、官僚、政党は関与するが、その分野に詳しいごく一部の者に過ぎない。一般市民はほとんど関与しなかった。また、法律が成立すると、行政が通達やガイドライン（ソフトロー）を作り、民間団体もこれに合わせてガイドラインを作り、国民はこれを官の命令として批判の余地無く遵守している状況である。日本では、欧米の法を若干保守的に制定し、さらにソフトローで保守的に運用する傾向にある。

このような状況の中で、学者やマスコミは、ハードローとは法的拘束力のあるものであるが、ソフトロー（行政や民間のガイドラインなど）は法的拘束力がないと説明してきた。

ソフトロー自体を「法の支配」の実質化の対象として扱ってこなかった。つまり、国民は法的拘束力のないものを守る必要もないから、有識者は長い間、ほとんど検討の対象にしてこなかった。しかし、国民にとっては日々接しているソフトローを守らざるを得ず、時代に合わせて積極的に改善することが必要でも、個人では何もなし得なかった。すなわち、日本国民は一般的には決められたルールを守るどころか、過剰に守ると言われてきた。なぜなら、江戸時代には、直訴（官への陳情）で獄門さらし首、明治になってもしきたりに違反すれば村八分、昭和になっても業界団体内の規律違反は、出入り禁止（取引停止）となった。国民はハードロー、ソフトローの区別無く、悪法であってもまじめに遵守せざるを得ない状況に置かれてきた。確かに、税務通達は刑罰の根拠にもなり、団体の規則違反は除名という制裁となり、国民が考えている通り、ソフトローも法的拘束力があるというのが正しいことになる。

　民間団体がソフトローを改革し、また行政と協力してソフトローを変えていくことは極めて有意義な法の改革となる。学者が法的拘束力が無いと言い、ソフトローの重要性を放置してきたのは間違っていたことが明らかとなった。現に行政法学者は欧米における行政規則の拘束力を研究し、教科書でも、法的拘束力はあるとの見解に変更しつつある。中山信弘
(4)(5)

教授らの東京大学２１世紀ＣＯＥプログラムは、2004年から日本で初めて、ソフトローを多角的に分析し、成果を公表してきた。私も、５年前から明確に、ソフトローは法的拘束力がある(6)との論文や本を出し続けている。国民が身近に接触(a)(b)(c)(d)しているソフトローこそが重要な役割を果たしている。ハードローは抽象的であり、ソフトローこそ生きた法である。そしてソフトローが、憲法や法律に違反する時には守る必要は無い。また、悪いソフトローは変えていくべきである。行政や民間団体はソフトローを作り、試行してみて、ハードローを作る、変える、廃止するというボトムアップ方式が望ましい。ソフトローからの法の改革、すなわち「ソフトローデモクラシー」とも言うべきものが「応答的法への道」であり、「法の支配」の実質化と言える。

　トクヴィルは1835年、アメリカのデモクラシーの中心に、結社の自由があり、政党ばかりか民間団体の自主的な行動規範（ソフトロー）が最も重要であるとみた。日本では団体は行政の指導により、または寡占目的のために作られてきた歴史(7)があり、これを抜本的に改革しなければならない。最近に至るまで、団体や企業は多くの不祥事を起こし、マスコミの批判を浴び、また犯罪について警察の取締りを受けてきた。団体や企業は社会変動に合わせて、法の支配の実質化に貢献するように、自主規律をもって豊かなソフトロー作りをし、

健全化することにより、刑事事件を減少させ、「抑圧的法」から脱する事ができる。行政、団体、企業の活動が情報公開され、社会変化に対応して国民の意見が反映されることが法の発展である。そして、やむを得ず紛争が起これば、早期に民事司法で結着するという「自律的法」を進めていけば、新たな政策が現場から発進され、円滑に「応答的法」への移行も可能となるであろう。

IV 規制改革と民事司法の強化

日本では、1990年代に日米構造内題協議において、米国から日本市場の閉鎖性と排他性の改善が求められた。その結果、独占禁止法の強化、独占禁止法適用除外立法の廃止と共に、行政規制の緩和撤廃が推進された。1993年に行政手続法、1999年に行政機関情報公開法、2003年に個人情報保護法が制定された。市場経済の成長を支援する法令、民間経済を行政が支える情報化社会の法令が整っていった。民事司法の法制度の改革ができないままに、欧米に習い、自由経済と福祉国家の法整備がなされた。本書ではこれらのハードローの制度が不充分であることを指摘する。しかし、出来上がっているハードローさえ、積極的に運用できず、むしろ保守的に解釈し、消極的に後ろ向きに運用する日本人の思考方法や行動様式を改革すべきであることをテーマとする。つまり、ハードローを積極的に運用するためのソフトローを作ること、さ

らにソフトローを充実させることにより、新しいハードローを作るべきことを提唱する。

V　村上春樹「１Ｑ８４」

　日本のノーベル賞候補作家の村上春樹の小説「1Q84」は、世界的にベストセラーになり、文学として高く評価されている。しかし、私は文学の視点からではなく、法律家の視点からみて、村上が無意識のうちに日本の「法の支配」の遅れを見事に描いたものとして高く評価したい。[8]

　ドメスティックバイオレンスの女性被害者を救済するために、主人公（女性）は次々に加害者を針で殺害していく。他方で、日本で現れたカルト宗教団体や左翼集団が犯罪を犯し、自壊していく状況をからめて描いたが、ここでも法による救済は全く期待されていない。

　村上は、日本の法曹、警察、団体への信頼や期待をいささかも示していない。NPOや救済組織を含む広い意味での「法の支配」に対する幻想を捨て去ってしまっている。この余りに超現実主義の世界を描いたことにより、リアリズム的な文学の視点からは否定的評価を受けるのではないかと思う。悪いカルトを批判しながら、良い宗教的救済の結果をとった。悪いDVを否定し、良い暴力を肯定する。この勧善懲悪は、日本の大衆文学の歴史を引き継いだ点では大成功である。江戸時代より現在まで、日本では小説や映画で水戸黄門、大岡

裁き、座頭市、清水の次郎長（ヤクザ）など、良い役人、良いヤクザによる良い暴力が礼賛され、暴力に頼らざるをえない状況が、繰り返し描かれてきた。しかし、権力行使か自力救済かを問わず、そのような暴力による解決は、応急的対応策に過ぎず、中長期的な改善策ではない。それ故、村上の現代的な小説でも、「法の支配」が全く無視されたこと、大衆が無意識に同感を示していることに大きな危機感を持つ。先進国家では、暴力に頼るのではなく、人々の意見と行動により、社会システムを復元しなければならない。そのためには、人々の結びつき、交流、意見交換が重要となる。日本では社会問題についての白熱したディベート、ソクラティック対話が乏しいので、これを積極的にしなければならない。

　皆様には1Q84の世界を少しでも超えて、勇気を持って現実の社会に少しずつでも向き合って、民主主義を進めてもらいたい。本書では、日本の方々に「解決すべき課題」を提示すると共に、海外の皆様に「日本の現状」と「進むべき方向」を理解して頂くために、日本語と英語をもって公表する。

第1章
理想としての
「法システムの4段階ピラミッドモデル」

Ⅰ 応答的法への進展（実質的法の支配）

1. 図1ピラミッドモデル（刑事→民事→行政→自主規律）応答的法型

　序文に示したように、犯罪や紛争の予防は、様々な制度政策によるべきであるが、事後的な制裁としての刑事処罰は抑制されるべきであり、民事司法の制裁と救済は拡大させ、行政と民間は協力して予防に努めるべきである。よって、日本においては、図1の4段階のピラミッドモデル（応答的法型）を理想とする。図2の逆ピラミッドモデルが従前のものであり、図1の理想的モデルを目指すには、更なる改革が必要である。ピラミッドモデルとは、上から下へ「強制、法的制裁、法的拘束力」が質的に弱まっていくこと、各段階のシステムの担う「人的資源、法の領域、社会的機能」が量的に広がっていくことを示している。

2. 図2逆ピラミッドモデル（行政→中間団体→刑事→民事）形式法型

　日本は、1990年頃まで国家による産業育成が優先し、行政の許可・認可の事前規制、強い行政指導が行われ、官製迎合と言われるものを含み、独占禁止法は充分な役割を果たせなかった。あらゆる業界の団体、全国の地域の団体は、行政の指導を遂行する役割を担った。この秩序に違反しては、経

第1章 理想としての「法システムの4段階ピラミッドモデル」

済活動をなし得なかった。戦争、公害、薬害、原子力発電事故は、自由な言論が封鎖されたこのような体制の中で引き起こされたものである。これらの災禍を受けた被害者は、民事裁判によっては、充分に救済を受けられなかった。また、市民や中小企業が大企業や行政を相手に民事裁判で勝訴をすることも少なく、民事裁判の社会的役割は極めて小さかった。

　私の前著では「行政→刑事→民事→中間団体」としたが、上記のとおり改訂する。ヘイリー教授や井上達夫教授の「日本社会は法や権力ではなく、中間的共同体の非法的・非公式的な制裁力・統制力によって秩序づけられてきた」との見解に全面的に賛同するので、これを反映させる。行政・中間的共同体・刑事の制裁に依存することは、自由や人権を侵害する抑圧的法のシステムである。但し、戦後には、表面的には法令や通達が作られてきたので、形式法型と呼ぶこととする。[9][10]

3. 規制改革

　1990年頃から、欧米の影響を受け、行政の規制緩和の意見が多く出始め、2000年小泉純一郎首相（自由民主党）、竹中平蔵大臣により、規制改革が進められた。学者やジャーナリストは、「事前規制は不公正、不平等となる」、「紛争や犯罪が発生すれば事後制裁（刑事罰）・事後救済（民事救済）による解決による社会システムが良い」と説明した。

　しかし、この説明は誤りであり、以下の通りの説明が正し

【法システムのピラミッド】

I　応答的法型

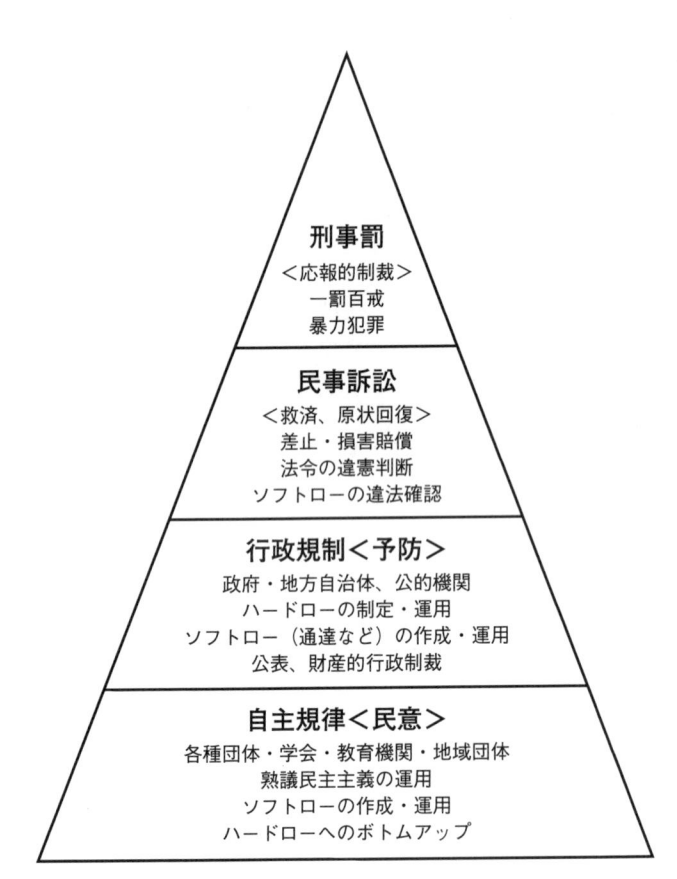

刑事罰
＜応報的制裁＞
一罰百戒
暴力犯罪

民事訴訟
＜救済、原状回復＞
差止・損害賠償
法令の違憲判断
ソフトローの違法確認

行政規制＜予防＞
政府・地方自治体、公的機関
ハードローの制定・運用
ソフトロー（通達など）の作成・運用
公表、財産的行政制裁

自主規律＜民意＞
各種団体・学会・教育機関・地域団体
熟議民主主義の運用
ソフトローの作成・運用
ハードローへのボトムアップ

第1章 理想としての「法システムの4段階ピラミッドモデル」

II 形式法型

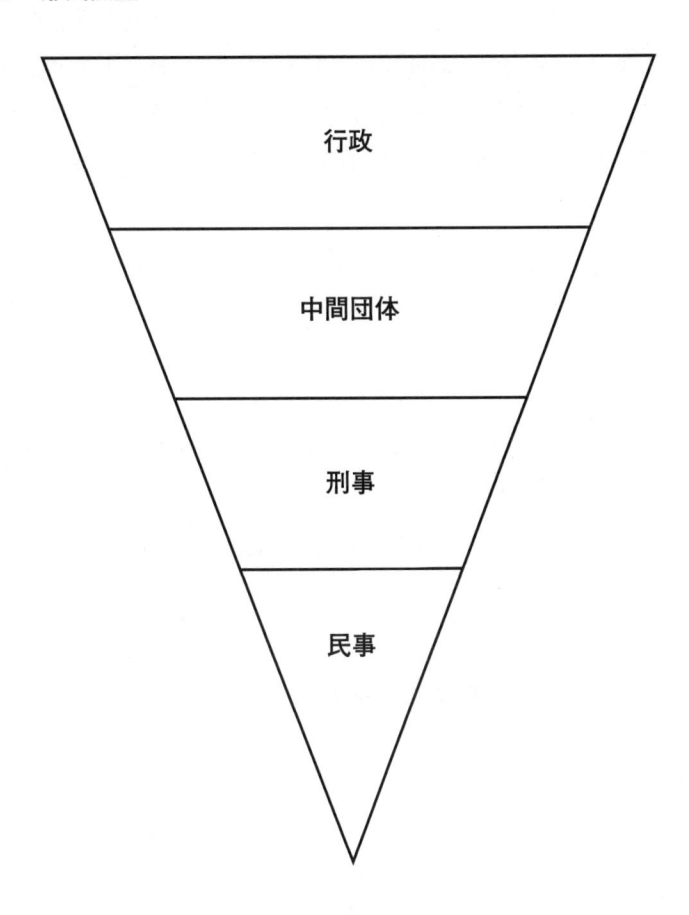

```
行政
中間団体
刑事
民事
```

い。

(1) 紛争や犯罪を予防することは、法システムの第1の目的である。行政や中間団体、市民がシステムを作り、常に改変していく必要がある。犯罪の範囲を拡大させ、厳罰主義をとっても予防にはならないし、システムを阻害する。米国のように公共政策の目的実現に民事訴訟を活用することも必要である。

(2) 引き起こされた被害を民事司法で救済することが第2の目的であり、米国のように民事システムを強化しなくてはならない。アスベスト被害の例をとれば、米国では訴訟により、北欧では行政立法により早期に救済を進めた。しかし、日本では主として訴訟により、補充的に行政立法によるが、救済は現在に至るまで著しく遅れている。

(3) これに対して犯罪者の制裁と隔離は最後の第3の手段である。

II 各段階の役割強化（改革）

1. 刑事

　日本では軽微な犯罪から市場や医療の犯罪まで余りに広く取締対象としてきた。徹底的に重点化すべきである。暴力事犯（殺人、強姦など）、北朝鮮の拉致などの取締を強化すべ

きである。他方で市場、医療などの分野に刑事権力は介入すべきでない。

2. 民事

民事裁判における証拠開示制度は不充分であり、真実を解明できない状況がある。そのため、賠償金額は安くなる傾向にある。また、被害者が賠償を求める立証の証明度が高いため、被害者救済は充分ではない。加害者を制裁するために、刑事司法に依存せず、民事裁判制度を強化することが必須である。

3. 行政（政府、自治体）

行政の予防機能を強化すべきである。従前は官僚（行政）が政治家、財界人と癒着し、経済活動に強固な規制を作ってきた。1990年頃から規制撤廃、規制改革が始まった。これに対して、逆に消費者、労働者、子供の安全を守るための予防的規制は強化すべきである。

4. 自主規律（民間）

従前は団体と学会は行政の指示に従い、かつ自らの利益を守るためのソフトロー作り（談合）をしてきた。しかし、今後は市民、消費者、労働者などの民意を反映させるためのソフトロー作りをするべきである。

Ⅲ 具体例

1. バブル経済崩壊の責任追及

　1990年のバブル経済の崩壊により、多くの銀行の巨額の貸出債権が不良債権化した。粉飾決算書を使って借り入れした不動産業者などの債務者が刑事処罰された。これはやむを得ない方法であった。しかし、銀行の役員が不良債権化することを明確には予期せず貸し付けた行為、公認会計士が粉飾決算を見抜けなかった行為、弁護士が債務者の資産譲渡に関与して、強制執行免脱とみられた行為などを起訴して刑事処罰したことは、全く誤っていた。大きな経済変動について必ずしも正確に予想できるものではない。経済活動についての刑事罰は、明白な故意、悪質な詐欺や脅迫などに限定すべきである。銀行の債権取り立て訴訟の効率化、迅速化など、民事裁判の改革こそ重要であった。ハードローの改革ばかりか、民事裁判手続きの運用の改善についてソフトローの改善こそ必要であったが、なし得なかった。

　税務上でも不良債権を直ちに損失とするとの運用もせず、前年度分の利益を繰り戻し還付する法律も停止させたままであった。公認会計士や弁護士については、各所属する団体で検討し、注意処分にすることで充分であった。多くの金融機関においては、役員は刑事処罰され、株主代表訴訟が提起さ

れ、巨額の損害賠償請求訴訟で敗訴した。私は和解や判決で役員の賠償額を分割化し、軽減すべきことを提案した。それにより、2006年に商法改正により会社役員の賠償額の上限(f)が定められるようになった。

2. 特定秘密保護法

2013年、公務員が国の秘密を指定できる法律が成立した。野党ばかりか、多くのジャーナリストや市民の強い反対を押し切った。法案の全ての条文が公表されたのは、衆議院での議決のわずか7日前であり、国民が議論する時間はなかった。条文は抽象的なものであった。

「法律」のみ成立させ、「これを具体化する施行令（政令）」、「運用を容易にするガイドライン」は同時に成立させていない。法の運用はソフトローであるガイドラインまで同時に成立させるのが理想である。法案では特定秘密の解除は、5年までに検討することとされた。ガイドラインで1週間、1ヶ月、3ヶ月、6ヶ月、1年などと決めることができるようにすれば、意見の大きな対立は縮小したはずである。

3. ハンセン病患者の損害賠償請求訴訟

日本では戦前から、患者を施設に厳しく隔離する政策が取られてきた。戦後、抗生物質により伝染しない状況になっても、1953年に「らい予防法」が制定され、隔離政策は変わらなかった。1996年、法律は廃止された。患者は1998年

に国家賠償訴訟を提訴し、2001年に勝訴判決を得た。患者、医師、地域住民、施設管理者は協力して、悪法を守らずに、徐々に解放処遇をするガイドラインを作り、実施すべきであった。全くそのような取り組みが無かった訳ではなく、支援者がいたからこそ、法律を廃止し、訴訟に勝利できた。しかし、悪法を乗り越えるソフトロー作りを意識的にすべき事案であり、その運動により、もっと早く、法律を死文化させるか、廃止できたのである。
(A)

4. 生殖補助医療

　一般的には社会は変化していくので、法令や倫理は遅れていく。法律や倫理に反する行為をするならば、刑事処罰、民事制裁、懲戒処分をうける。悪法といえども法とされる。悪法を無視して社会の要請に応える行為、正義を貫く行為を一人で行う時には、上記のような制裁を受けるリスクがある。菊田医師は、高校生の出産児を引き取る夫婦の実子として、出産証明書を記載したので、虚偽文書作成罪に問われ、優生保護法指定医（母体保護法指定医）の資格も剥奪された。飯塚理八医師（慶応大学教授）は1949年よりAIDを実施し、批判された。根津医師は、1999年精子と卵子の提供による体外受精を公表し、日本産科婦人科学会を除名された。日本産科婦人科学会の体外受精のガイドラインでは、医師は体外受精を夫婦の間でしか実施してはならないとされていた。大

谷医師は2004年、習慣流産（染色体異常）の患者に着床前診断をしたことが報道され、同じく除名となった。ガイドラインは、「重い遺伝性疾患」（筋ジストロフィーなど）に限定して許容していた。私は上記3人と共にフロム（妊娠出産をめぐる自己決定権を支える会）を立ち上げ、精子と卵子の提供、代理出産、着床前診断について、これらを認める運用方針（ソフトロー）を公表していった。

日本受精着床学会、日本生殖医学会も理解を始め、2013年に至り日本産科婦人科学会もガイドラインを柔軟に運用するようになった。精子卵子提供と代理出産については、これを認める新法が準備されるに至っている。

Ⅳ　ソフトロー・デモクラシー

1. ハードロー

　日本の国会（衆議院と参議院）の制定する法律、地方議会の制定する条例はハードローである。代表制民主主義を核とする立憲主義において最高の権威と正当性を有する議会が制定する。よって手続きが厳格で、法的拘束力は強く、改変は困難である。しかし、ハードローの文言は抽象的であるので、ソフトローにより具体的に解釈や運用を変えていけるので、短期の改変は必要ない。

2. ソフトロー

　ソフトローとは、本来国際法を指し、国家の強制力をもたない法とされ、法的拘束力はない、または弱いとされてきた。しかし、EUの発展において、ソフトローの果たした役割は極めて大きい。本書では「議会」以外で定められる以下のルールをソフトローとして扱う。一般的には、下記（1）は法的根拠と拘束力の明白性からハードローと言われており、ソフトローとは言わない。しかし、行政立法に過ぎず、改変が容易であるのでソフトローとして扱う。下記（2）（3）は、一般的には法的拘束力がないと言われているが、様々な法的効力が認められる。行政ソフトローに違反すると、刑罰を受け、民間ソフトローに違反すると除名や損害賠償請求を受けることがある。法的拘束力の根拠は、行政組織や民間団体における多数決決定、合意、組織決定であり、ハードローの形成手続と大きくは変わらない。

（1）法規命令（行政の制定）

　　　　政令—内閣の制定する施行令

　　　　省令—各省大臣の制定する施行規則

（2）行政規則（行政ソフトロー）、行政指導

（3）民間ソフトロー（公益団体ソフトロー、民間団体ソフトロー）

3. 代表制デモクラシーの限界

　代表者を選挙で選ぶ議会制民主主義は、直接民主主義ではなく、間接民主主義である。市民は選挙の時には意思を表示できるが、政党や議員が民意を反映できるかは疑問とされるに至った。議会制民主主義は人々の生活と福祉を守れるか、経済を発展させられるかも不安視されている。また、特定の項目について市民が改革を望んでも、市民が直接法律を作ることはできない。人々がハードローを作ったり、改変したり、廃止したりすることは極めて困難である。市民から見てハードローは遠い彼方に存在するものである。市民が代表制デモクラシーに期待を持たなくなり、投票に行く人も減少する傾向になる。他の様々なデモクラシーが追求されている。
(12)

4. ソフトローの活用（ボトムアップ）

　民間ソフトローは市民に極めて身近なものである。市民自らが制定したり、改変する事が容易といえる。行政ソフトローはハードローより改変する事は容易である。日本では古い行政ソフトローが山のようにあり、経済活動の自由を制約している。約15年ほど前までは、一度作られたものを改変する事は困難であった。しかし、規制改革の進展、民主党政権への移行により、行政ソフトローの改変も多くなった。NPO、NGO、中間団体の請願運動、署名活動などによることが多い。しかし、中間団体自身のソフトロー作成により試行や実
(13)

験をしつつ、行政ソフトローを変えていくことが理想といえる。民間ソフトローから行政ソフトローへ、そしてハードローの改変へとボトムアップしていくのがソフトローデモクラシーである。2009年に、ジョン・キーンは現代の世界中のモニタリングデモクラシーを紹介したが、ソフトローデモクラシーはその中に含まれるものとして最も核と言える。なぜなら、ソーシャルネットワーク、デモ行進などは情報発信[14]としては重要だが、法という規範に高まるとは限らないからである。

5. ソフトローの特性と効用

（1）ソフトローには以下の特性がある。
 1．柔軟性（ある程度緩やかに解釈すること）
 2．可変性（状況に応じて、容易に変えられること、手続が簡単ということ）
 3．暫定性（とりあえず決めておくという趣旨。社会の状況に応じて、臨時的に措置をしておくという意味）
 4．多様性（地域、団体により異なったものでもよいということ）

（2）ソフトローを作成したり、改訂していく上で、下記のことが重要となる。
 1．情報
 　情報を収集し、関係者に開示すること

第1章　理想としての「法システムの4段階ピラミッドモデル」

2．討議
　　上記の正確な様々な情報を分析し、関係者が討議すること
3．新しい案の公表
　　上記の討議に基づいて、新しい案を公表し、更に意見を求めること
4．実施
　　上記の新しい案に基づいて、実際に実施すること
5．事前通知
　　事前にマスコミに公表し、社会に伝達していくこと。また、刑事罰に関係する場合には、警察に届け出ておくこと

（3）悪法に従わず、ソフトローを含めて良い法を作ろうとする姿勢は、以下の通りの効用がある。

①法が良いか悪いかを常に検討する姿勢を持つことができる。

②与えられたものとして金科玉条に守ることがなくなる。
　上から決められたことを鵜呑みにすることがなくなる。

③新しいやり方があるかどうか、常に考えるようになる。

④良い法か悪い法か、新しい法は何か、常に議論することができる。

⑤民間団体や役所の中の自由な討議を保障するために、民

主的手続や組織の民主制が保たれることになる。

⑥常に正確な情報を収集するようになる。

⑦情報を常に開示し、透明性を高めることができる。

⑧官尊民卑の弊害をなくす。

⑨ボトムアップ方式であり、民意を反映することができる。

⑩公務員や国会議員の役に立つような、新しい法案を提示することができる。

⑪悪い法を廃止し、良い法を作ることは、自分の利益だけではなく、常に公益のためになることを意識する。

6. 裁判所の判決

　日本には、ドイツ、韓国の憲法裁判所は存在しない。最高裁判所の違憲立法審査権は、米国と同じに個別事件において法律の条文そのものを無効にできる点で、ハードローの持つ強い拘束性を超えるものである。これに対して、それ以外の判決は必ずしも絶対的ではない。

（1）地方裁判所、高等裁判所の違憲立法審査権といえども、最高裁の判決が出るまでのもので、多様性、暫定性を持っている。ソフトローと同じ面がある。

（2）地裁から最高裁まで、判決は法令の解釈、法令の適用を行っている。判決毎に可変性、多様性、暫定性があり、ソフトローの性質を持つ。社会変動に適合する法の解釈、法の当てはめを積極的、合目的的にすべき点では、ソフトローの

運用と同じように考えるべきと言える。

(3) 研究者と裁判官として著名であった瀬木比呂志は、裁判官退職直後の2014年に「絶望の裁判所」を公表し、「日本の裁判所は、最高裁事務総局が支配し、旧ソ連のような全体主義的共産主義体制に非常に似ており、憲法で保障されているはずの裁判官の独立もなく、判決では、人権や正義を守るどころか、保守的な結論を決めておいて、形式的な理由をつけるものがほとんどである」、「官僚裁判官を廃止し、弁護士から裁判官になる法曹一元にすべし」と主張する。

2000年度に実施された調査によれば、民事裁判を利用した人々が訴訟制度に対して満足していると答えた割合は、わずかに18.6％にすぎず、それが利用しやすいと答えた割合も、わずかに22.4％にすぎないというアンケート結果が出ている。
(16)
このような状況を変えるには、有識者を始めとする国民全体が、法の運用がいかに重要であるかを認識し、少しずつ改善していかなければならない。日本では、判決においても、先例踏襲主義が行きすぎたものとなっている。ソフトローと同じに、柔軟に変えていかなければならない。

(4) 黒木亮は、2013年、正確な取材に基づきノンフィクションというべき小説「法服の王国―小説裁判官」の中で、最高裁事務総局により不当な転勤や配転をテコに、裁判官の独立

が犯されていく状況と、多くの反原発訴訟が住民側敗訴となる状況を描いた。上記瀬木の報告と合わせれば、1999年から２年間の司法改革審議会(17)のときに、裁判官が若干の積極主義になったが、すぐに裁判所内部の抑圧的法に戻ったといえる。

第 2 章
刑事裁判システムの改革

I 重点化と代替案

1. 暴力事犯

　日本の警察と検察は、戦前から1970年頃まで社会主義勢力（労働者、学生）を主たる取締りの対象とした。その後は国民の活動のあらゆる分野に介入してきた。それにも関わらず、暴力事犯の取締、特に暴力団の根絶に至らなかった。暴力団対策法（1991年）による取締でも充分ではなく、2012年の全県の暴力団排除条例により、暴力団員と密接関係者との関係切断を市民の義務とし、更に強化している。但し、諸外国のように暴力団禁止法には至っていない。また、北朝鮮による拉致、オウム真理教の大量殺人、ストーカー殺害など、絶え間ない暴力事犯が発生してきた。約600件の未解決事件があると言われている。

　他方で戦後だけでも、20年〜40年の拘禁の後に判明したものも含めて、約10件の冤罪の再審決定があり、司法の威信が揺らいでいる。警察の人員とコストをより多く、暴力事犯に振り向けて重点化すべきは明らかである。

2. 市場と医療への過剰介入

　1970年代から、警察の取締り対象は、悪徳商法の大規模詐欺事件、公害、経済犯などに広がっていった。1990年にバブル経済の崩壊が始まり、デフレ経済が現在まで続いた。[18]

銀行の過大な貸付は巨額の不良債権となった。銀行の幹部が次々に逮捕され、有罪とされた。また、上場企業の粉飾決算が発生し、役員や公認会計士が有価証券虚偽記載罪として刑事処罰された。さらに医療過誤において医師が逮捕され、有罪とされた。このように、企業人、公認会計士、弁護士、医師、看護師が逮捕され有罪とされた。

しかし、有罪とされた者は一般的業務活動をしており、客観的にも主観的にも犯罪者とは言えなかった。もちろん、最も悪質な者を一罰百戒のために起訴することもありえたが、悪質でない者を起訴したことで一部は無罪となり、増々社会的混乱を強めた。有罪とされた者も同じように法令違反した多くの者のごく一部に過ぎなかった。

これらの問題の予防や解決は刑事処罰に頼るのではなく、他の手段によるべきである。民事裁判、団体の自主規律により、予防や解決をすべきである。社会的ジレンマの研究によれば、集団が小さいほど、コミュニケーションが取れ、協調的行動が多くなるという。協調行動の相互促進が重要となる。[19]そのためには、団体や地域における小集団毎のソフトロー[20]作りから始めるべきである。

3. ソフトローによる企業犯罪対策

悪質な企業犯罪、暴力団の絡む取引犯罪については、刑事処罰による企業やグループの解体が必要である。他方で、一

般企業に対しては、消費者・投資者・労働者を保護する法令、環境・衛生を守る法令などを遵守させるには、環境犯罪学の手法により、監視を含む予防措置などの環境（状況）を整え、刑事処罰に依存しないで、様々な手段を組み合わせる必要がある。

犯罪学者J・ブレイスウェイトの提案した「強制された自主規制」(Enforced Self-Regulation)は、日本の就業規則のように、企業に固有な状況に適したルールを作らせ、規制当局の承認の下に監督を受けつつ実施させるものである。同教授は、応答的規制（responsive regulation）として様々な代替案を示し、また事後においても、刑罰によらない修復的司法（restorative justice）を評価する。

また、米国では、組織体に対する連邦量刑ガイドライン（1991年）に合わせて、企業内のコンライアンス・プログラムの作成と実施により、予防と刑罰軽減を行う体制が進んだ。日本でも、内部統制マニュアルやパワハラ・セクハラ防止マニュアルなどの犯罪予防の整備が進んだ。上記はいづれも企業内部で自主的に健全なソフトローを作ることであり、刑事罰を回避するに必要な手法である。

さらに、企業内の個人を刑事処罰してもあまり有効でない。企業自体を改革させるための制度として、企業の役員が違法行為をしたときには、金融商品取引法や医療法には、行政庁

が役員を解任（勧告）できるとの重要な規定がある。法令に規定がないときには、企業や団体の定款に規定しておく手法が有効といえる。

4. 給付行政の適正化

　福祉国家において膨大な社会保障費が交付され、詐欺的な不正受給が拡大している。景気刺激策の公共事業のための財政出費でも、不正受給が横行している。全てを刑事処罰で取り締ることはできない。内部告発制度を活用するなど効率化、適正化すべきである。

Ⅱ　刑事実務の後進性（抑圧性）（4つの欠陥の改革）

1. 保釈の拡大（人質司法の解消）

　刑事訴訟法 89 条の趣旨は、逃亡の恐れのないこと、証拠隠滅の恐れのない場合には、被疑者を保釈をしなければいけないとされている。条文では、自白をした場合には保釈できるとも書かれていないし、自白をしない場合には保釈をできないとも書かれていない。しかるに、自白をしない場合には、逮捕から約 23 日間の勾留、さらに起訴後勾留を含め、2、3 ヵ月に及ぶことがある。第 1 回公判後も自白をしないとさらに勾留が続くことがある。保釈の運用は、完全に違法の状態となっている。人質司法とは、警察や検察が身柄を人質にした

上で、自白を強要し、自白をしたら保釈をするという運用である。今後は、起訴後直ちに否認していても保釈を認めるように、弁護士会と裁判所は運用改善について協議すべきである。逮捕から3日後からの勾留期間中の保釈制度は立法化すべきである。

2. 取調の可視化（自白調書偏重）

日本では、江戸時代から「自白は証拠の王」とされてきた。第二次大戦前は拷問が常態化しており、戦後も暴力による取り調べ、さらには精神的虐待が続いてきた。長時間の取調と家族や関係者の逮捕などを材料に強迫し、自白を取ってきた。現在までテープレコーダーによる録音はされてこなかった。2010年、検察官の証拠ねつ造事件（検察官3名の逮捕・起訴）により、刑事捜査への強い批判が高まり、取調可視化の検討が始まっている。しかし、現在の法制審議会の検討でも、先進諸国で行われている取調べの全面的可視化の結論は出されていない。

3. 全面証拠開示の実現

検察と警察は強制的に証拠を集めることができる。この証拠は、国民の財産であり、裁判においてはすべて開示されなければならない。しかし、日本では、検察が有罪立証に有利なもののみを開示する。1969年、最高裁は、個別開示方式を認め、裁判所は狭い範囲で開示命令を出してきた。当事者

対等を原則とする憲法や法律に違反している。2001年、司法改革審議会報告書は、裁判員裁判導入と共に証拠開示制度の法制化を提言した。2004年に条文化されたが、諸外国で見られる「無罪証拠へのアクセス権」、「検察官の無罪証拠開示義務」を採用していないという不完全なものである。[25]

4. Beyond a reasonable doubt の採用

　日本では最高裁判決（1975年）や、学者の刑事訴訟法の書物では、「推定無罪」「疑わしきは罰せず」「高度の蓋然性の証明」とし、米国と同じに「Beyond a reasonable doubt が原則である」とされている。しかし、明確には、日本の刑事裁判官に浸透していない。「真の犯罪者を逃しても冤罪を出してはならない」との原則が徹底されていない。警察は犯人逮捕の公表を優先してしまい、公表した後には、検事と裁判官がこれをくつがえすことは、ほとんど出来ない状況が続いてきた。有罪率は99.99％以上であったところ、裁判員裁判において無罪率が上昇したことから、官僚裁判官の「有罪推定」の立場が明らかとなった。

Ⅲ　欠陥を是正できない理由

1. 警察と検察

　治安優先、刑事依存の法システムが続いてきた。

社会的危機を一部の人をスケープゴートにして、鎮静化させる厳罰化ポピュリズムが繰り返し常態化している。

2. 特捜検察

検察庁の中の特別捜査本部は、特に重要事件を警察と共に、または警察と別に扱う。政治家や官僚を逮捕、勾留し、刑事制裁をし、健全な法社会とみせようとしたが、強引な捜査方法が批判されるようになった。特にバブル崩壊による社会混乱を刑事処罰で納めようとしたことは、国の経済運営の失敗の責任を転化させる面があった。

3. 学界の意見

戦後は団藤、田宮、平野らの多くの学者が欧米の人権保障の様々なシステムを紹介してきたが、実務にほとんど反映されていない。

4. 検察改革

「検察の在り方検討会議」及び「新時代の刑事司法制度特別部会」などにおいて、有識者が参加し、検察、刑事司法の改革が検討された。すべての事件での取調の全面可視化、全面証拠開示までの結論に至っていない。

Ⅳ 裁判員裁判

裁判員裁判（裁判官3名、裁判員6名）は2009年から始

まった。5年間の実施により、今後の改善が検討され始めている。

1. 無罪率の上昇 (26)

以前の裁判官のみの裁判では、無罪率は0.01％以下であったが、裁判員裁判では約0.5％（30/6000）となり無罪率が高まり、一定の成果があげられている。

2. 被告人の選択権

裁判員裁判は、少数の重罪事件のみに限定して強制されている。罪の軽重を問わず、被告人の権利として選択できるように改革すべきである。

3. 評議の秘密

裁判員の秘密保持義務（刑罰）が厳しいため、裁判員裁判の検証をしにくいこと、裁判員の精神的負担が重いことが問題となっている。検証を目的とする団体でソフトローにより徐々に解禁していく方法がありうる。

第3章
民事裁判の改革

I 民事裁判の欠陥

1. 被害救済の強化の必要性

　不正行為、契約違反、法令違反行為から被害を受けた者を迅速に救済し、金銭賠償を得させることが、民事裁判の目的である。しかし、日本では民事訴訟の発展が遅れ被害者の救済が充分でなかった。

　日本の民事裁判制度は約 100 年前にドイツの制度を模して作られた。自由主義的な当事者対等の訴訟法であり、武器(金、証拠)を持つ強者の方が弱者より有利な法であった。しかし、ドイツではその後、社会的経済的弱者たる市民や労働者を救済する社会的民事訴訟またはシュトゥットガルト・モデルが発展した。職権主義または協働主義による「立証責任の転換、過失の推定、証拠提出命令の拡大」へと大きく改革された。しかし、日本では研究者がすべて紹介したが、改革されなかった。
[e]
　米国でも民事裁判は、ディスカバリーの拡大と共に爆発的発展を遂げた。しかし、日本では米国の司法積極主義、応答的法を支える当事者対抗的リーガリズムの下記制度は存在しない。
[27]
(1) 民事陪審
(2) ディスカバリー

(3) 懲罰賠償 (punitive damage)、3 倍賠償 (treble damage)
(4) クラスアクション
(5) 証拠の優越（preponderance of evidence)、（日本では原告の被害者に 70 ～ 80%の高い証明責任が課せられている）

　結論として欧米に比べて民事裁判の機能は弱く、紛争解決は刑事処罰に依存する傾向となっていた。

2. 証拠開示の拡大の必要性

　裁判制度の核心は、事実の解明をした上での、真偽の判断である。そのためには、証拠の全面開示が必要となる。旧民事訴訟法の文書提出命令は 4 つの制限類型しか認めなかった。私と少数の学者は米国のディスカバリーの導入を主張した。また、私は次善の策として、当事者の陳述書、関係者の報告書の提出により、事実の開示を進める改善案を提示し、裁判所は大幅にこれを採用し、ソフトローによる一大改革がなされた。1996 年に民事訴訟法の条文は改正され、原則として文書提出命令は広く認められることとなった。しかし、その後の裁判所の運用は大きく変わらず、事案解明がされないままに以下の通り、不充分な判決が出される状況が続いている。

(1) 裁判官は証拠が多くなると負担が大きくなるので、必要最小限にしぼっている。

(2) 当事者が「紛失した、存在しない、破棄した」といえば提出命令を出さない。
(3) 裁判官は「必要性がない」として却下する。日本では、文書に限らず、証人尋問、検証、鑑定など全て「必要性が無い」として却下できる制度となっている。却下の理由を告知する必要はなく、これについて不服申立手続もない。しかし、文書については簡易に証拠調べできるのであり、裁判所の統一した運用の実務(ソフトロー)は憲法違反となっている。

Ⅱ 分割責任の拡大の必要性

1. 不法行為法での拡大

　日本では交通戦争と言われるほどの交通事故の多発があった。車社会では人々は加害者にも被害者にもなりうる状況であった。また、被害者側にも原因や責任があることも多かった。そこで、過失相殺により割合的に責任を分割する判決が多くなった。弁護士会が中心となり、保険会社、裁判所の意見も聴取[c]しながら過失相殺の多くの類型を図形で示した。ソフトローとして定着した。但し、酒酔い運転による悲惨な人身事故が続いたため、危険運転致死傷罪、自動車運転過失致傷罪などにより厳罰化法案が成立した。

2. 契約法と信義誠実原則

　不正行為の領域全般において、過失相殺の解決方法が広まった。しかしながら、契約法の領域では過失相殺の考え方が採用されない。たとえば、代理人の取引のケースで本人と取引相手方に双方に責任がある事案が多発しているが、100か0かの不合理な判決が続いている。民法第1条の「信義誠実の原則」を使用すれば、妥当な結論を得られるが、法形式主義を脱しられない。[28]
(c)

Ⅲ　法政策機能強化の必要性

1. 社会的責任から法的責任へ（米国）

　ノネとセルズニックによれば、米国では自律的法を超え、応答的法が司法積極主義（judicial activism）として、公共政策の目的を追求した社会的弁護（social advocacy）の噴出の下に発展した。

　R・A・ケイガンは、米国の法社会を当事者対抗的リーガリズム（adversarial legalism）と呼ぶ。「政策の形成・実施が、[29] 官僚行政によるのではなく、弁護士支配的な訴訟を通じてなされること」とし、司法は新種の訴訟や政治運動に対して開かれているという。この米国司法の発展は、被害者救済の社会的責任が法的責任にまで高められ、具体化していく歴史で

あった。コモンローの救済では不充分となり、エクイティ上の広い救済が進められた。そして、公共政策の実現のツールともなった。

2. 行政への不介入（日本）

　日本でも既に 1988 年に米国の法の発展を、「制度改革訴訟」を含む「現代型訴訟または公共訴訟」として紹介された。しかし、日本では、裁判所は、行政の分野に介入しないとの立場に立ち、行政を相手とする訴訟は 99％以上敗訴し、法創造の発展は見られなかった。東京地裁行政部裁判長藤山雅行は、極めて例外的に多くの行政側敗訴の判決を出したが、上級審で変更された。

第4章
行政規制（予防）

I　予防的機能

　刑事システムでは事後的に犯罪者を制裁する。民事システムでは事後的に被害者を救済する。事前に犯罪を予防したり、被害発生を防ぐには、行政による予防的機能に頼らざるをえない。従前、行政（政府、自治体）は、政党と共に産業の育成、財政出動、社会保障などの立法案を作成し国会で成立させ、実施することを主たる役割としてきた。法律の執行は、行政府がトップダウンで実行し、具体化はほとんど通知や通達で行われ、通達行政と言われた。

　これに対して、公害、PL、交通事故、労災、投資被害、災害などについて、予防的立法は極めて遅れた。公害を防ぐための環境省の成立は2001年（平成13年）になり、消費者の安全を守るための消費者庁の成立は2009年（平成21年）となった。事後的に金銭的救済をする法律はいくつか成立したが、予防的機能は充分に果たされていない。最近では、原子力災害、地球温暖化、資源乱開発、環境破壊、戦争、テロなど、グローバルな形で世界的リスクが発生している。人類が引き起こしている点で人災だが、津波被害も含めて、発生前の予防、発生後の措置のいずれにおいても人災の面が強い(31)と言われている。行政を中心とする予防システムを強化する必要があり、以下の方法を進めるべきである。

第4章　行政規制（予防）

1. 予防的立法

　法律により、抽象的には市民、消費者、労働者などの安全を予防すべきことが可能とされている。しかし、具体的な因果関係の証明無しに予防措置をとれない。そこで、予防のための抑止措置としては行政処分（勧告、是正命令、停止命令）と公表制度を組み合わせることとなる。被害の発生についての原因が高度の蓋然性で証明できない場合でも、50％～60％前後の証明度をもって、規制できることを明確にするべきである。

2. ソフトロー

　抽象的な法律の条文を具体的に解釈し、運用するためにソフトロー（ガイドライン）を活用するべきである。証明度が90％などに高まれば厳しく規制し、証明度が55％などと低い時には緩やかに規制するなど、柔軟に、可変的に運用できる。

3. 予防のための抑止措置

　証明度の低い時には勧告、公表により、証明度が高い場合には違反行為の是正命令、営業の停止命令を出せる事とする。立法によれば、この命令に違反する時に刑事罰を加えることができる。勧告（注意処分）だけであれば、対象者に具体的制約は発生しない。しかし、ほとんどの場合公表されることにより、社会的制裁を受ける。是正命令、停止命令により具

体的制約が発生し、公表されることにより、更に制裁的効果が発生する。

II　行政ソフトローの大きな展開

1. 外部化現象

　日本においては、国会で法律が制定された後に、政令（内閣）や省令（大臣）が作成される。「法規命令」であり、法的拘束力を有する。これに対して通達、通知、要綱、告示などは、「行政規則」と呼ばれ、公務員に対してのみ法的拘束力（内部効果）はあるが、国民に対する法的拘束力（外部効果）はないとされてきた。しかし、最近では法的拘束力があるとの考え方（外部化現象）が強くなり、ガイドラインや指針という名称が多くなった。1997年、臓器移植について「臓器移植に関する法律」「臓器移植に関する法律の施行規則」「ガイドライン」と、ハードローとソフトローが同時に作られた。

　行政規則は先例踏襲（自己拘束）、平等原則、予測性から法的拘束力を付与されたもので、ハードローの原理と変わりはない。しかし、行政立法（法規命令・行政規則のソフトロー）は、議会の法（ハードロー）とは異なり、現代社会では状況に合わせ、可変性、暫定性、多様性を有すべきである。先例踏襲、平等原則、予測性を減少させても、ソフトローの

特性を生かすべきである。また、「行政指導」も世界で初めて 1993 年に行政手続法に明文化され、ソフトローとして認知された。行政ソフトローも、組織決定であることにより、法的拘束力が生じる。

2. 公表

　通達や通知は公表されなかったために、特別な関係者しか知らないことも多く、一般国民が広くこれを検討することもできなかった。1993 年の行政手続法により公表が義務付けられた。21 世紀に入りインターネットが普及したことにより、行政庁の制定する通達やガイドラインを、ほとんど知ることができるようになった。そのため、ガイドライン制定のときから、その後の変更の検討にも十分に手続をとることができるようになった。

Ⅲ　行政ソフトローの民主的運用

　長い間、行政ソフトローは官僚の一方的かつ閉鎖的運用がされた。また、年と共に社会に適合しなくなり、放置されてしまうものも多い。そして、ハードローと異なり、具体化されればされる程、矛盾が生じたり、空白部分も明らかとなる。これらに対応し、民意を反映する手続が作られた。

1. 行政手続法

　国及び地方公共団体の行政運営における「公正の確保」と「透明性の向上」をはかるために1993年に行政手続法が成立した。この法律により、行政手続（許認可や行政指導）において、行政庁は申請の審査基準を定め、それを公にすることが義務付けられた。不利益処分の前には「理由の提示」がされることとなり、処分を受ける者の権利利益を保護するために「聴聞手続」が保障された。

　「行政指導」についても、口頭だけでなく、市民から「書面交付請求」ができるようになった。行政のソフトローの運用が透明化されたため、各種団体はこれをめぐり大いに議論し、よりよいソフトローへと改善できることとなった。

2. パブリック・コメント手続き（意見公募手続き）[32]

　ソフトローは社会状況の変化に応じて、迅速に作ったり、柔軟に改変することができることが特徴である。トップダウンの通達行政を改善するため、パブリック・コメント手続き（意見公募手続き）は、1999年に閣議決定され、2005年に改正行政手続法第6章に法制化された。ソフトローが制定されるときまたは改変されるときに、利害関係人だけでなく、一般市民を含めて広く意見を求めるものである。対象も国民の権利または義務に直接関る「命令等」（行政指導まで含む）に広げられた。

第4章　行政規制（予防）

　原田久教授は約１０年に渡る手続きの実証検証を行った。①パブリック・コメント手続が実施される件数が少ないこと、②手続１件にあたり寄せられる意見数が少ないこと、③意見を受けて修正に至る割合が低いことが課題であった。これに対し、改革案としては①重点化、②能働化、③透明化が必要であるとした。[33]

3. 法令適用事前申請確認手続

　これはアメリカのノーアクションレターを参考に導入された。法律ではなく、2000年の閣議決定により定められたものである。

「民間企業等が、実現しようとする自己の事業活動に係る具体的行為に関して、当該行為が特定の法令の規定の適用対象となるかどうかを、あらかじめ当該規定を所轄する行政機関に確認し、その機関が回答を行うとともに、当該回答を公表する手続きの指針を下記のとおり定める」とされている。

　法令の解釈について、回答がおかしいと考えれば各種団体で別の解釈論を作り所轄官庁と協議できる、つまり、ソフトローの自由な討議が可能になった。

Ⅳ　行政ソフトローに対する民事的コントロール

　行政の運用基準（ソフトロー）を、新しい時代に向けて改

革していくには、官と民の協力により円滑に変えていくのが理想的であるが、合わせて裁判所の積極的役割を必要とする。

1. 無効確認と差止請求（行政の裁量権の限界）

　戦前には、裁判所は行政の自由裁量行為については、審査自体をしないという原則であった。しかし、戦後、行政事件訴訟法30条により、裁判所は、行政処分が、「裁量権の踰越または濫用のあるとき」、すなわち「社会通念上著しく妥当性を欠くとき」には、これを取り消すことが出来ることとなった。しかし、原告の取消請求訴訟は全くといっていいほど、認められなかった。

　1993年、行政手続法の制定により、処分庁により審査基準・処分基準が作成され、公にされることになり、司法審査が拡充された。2004年には、行政事件訴訟法が改正され、義務付訴訟、差止訴訟が新設された。

　例として、日本では戦争前からの国旗と国歌を変えなかったため、社会問題が起きたものを挙げる。公立学校の教員に、通達で「国旗への起立、国歌の斉唱とピアノ伴奏」を命令し、これに反した者を減給や停職の処分としたところ、多くの取消訴訟が起こされた。原告は地裁で1部勝訴したが、最高裁ではすべて敗訴した。その内で、特筆すべきは、事前に「起立・斉唱・伴奏の義務のないことの確認請求」（通達の無効確認）と「処分の差止請求」を認める画期的地裁判決が出されたこ

とである。原告らが懲戒処分などを受ける前の民事訴訟であり、裁判所がこれを認めたことは過去の判例に比べ画期的である。紛争について予防的機能を発揮して、通達の無効確認を前提として救済を認めた。反対運動への刑事弾圧や懲戒処分の前に解決する予防的救済司法の誕生である。しかし、原告は、高裁、最高裁（2012年）では逆転敗訴し、請求は認められなかった。結論として、法制度は進歩しているが、法の運用は停滞しているといえる。
(B)

但し、医薬品のインターネット販売が現実に広まる中で、対面販売を強制する行政指導について、原告の業者がインターネット販売の禁止は薬事法の委任の範囲を超えて無効であることの確認請求をしたところ、2013年に最高裁はこれを認めたので、わずかに前進したと言える。
(C)

2. 国家賠償請求訴訟

原告が勝訴することは極めて少ない状況である。公務員が行政規則に従っている限り、仮に行政規則が違法または無効とされても、国には原則として国家賠償法に基づく損害賠償義務がない。しかし、行政規則が、相対的弾力的なものであることから、公務員は硬直的運用をしない義務を負い、国民に対し損害を与えないようにする義務がある。そこで行政規則が違法ないし無効となった場合には、あるいは公務員に運用についての違法があるとき、国または自治体に不法行為と

しての損害賠償義務が発生する。しかし、その場合には公務員個人の行為ではなく、組織としての継続的な責任が問われるものであり、法人としての不法行為と考えなければならない。日本では、公務員個人の責任は悪意でもない限り、一切問われない運用となっている。

第5章
自主規律（自己統治）

I　民間ソフトローの役割

1. 中間団体の新しい役割

　1835年トクヴィルは、王制や貴族制に代わる社会の単位として、個人ではなく、政治的結社と市民的結社を必須のものとした。この結社の自由を陪審と共にアメリカのデモクラシーの基礎ととらえた。また、1994年ポール・ハーストは、結社民主主義を主張した。[7]

　立法、行政、司法という国家機関以外に、民間の組織がソフトローを形成し、運用している。経済社会の変動、法令の改変に合わせて、民間のソフトローも柔軟に変えていかなければならない。担い手は中間団体と総称するが、以下の通り膨大な数がある。[34]

公益団体（職業団体、専門家団体、労働組合連合会、学会など）
地域団体（自治会、町会、マンション組合など）
民間組織（企業、労働組合、PTAなど）

　従前の中間団体は、自らの既得権益を守るために活動し、行政と共に参入規制をするために、ソフトローを形成してきた。しかし、現在では憲法上の保障である「経済活動の自由」を守り、消費者を保護するために、行政規制の縮小と独禁法

の強化が進んでいる。但し、今でも最も厚い岩盤規制を担うのは、全国農業協同組合連合会、電力企業連合会、日本医師会と言われており、その他にも多くの参入規制団体が残っている。そこで、今や中間団体は、規制改革に合わせて独占的利益を得ることをやめ、消費者及び市民の利益や安全のためにソフトローを運用する義務が生じている。業界団体も、自主規制により公益を守ることを始めている。
(35)

2. ソフトローの社会適合機能

ソフトローは、一般的には法令を具体的に運用するための解釈規定、実施規定といえる。しかし、現在の日本で最も重要な役割は、社会変動と経済発展に柔軟に適合するルール作りである。法律は年数が立てば社会に適合しなくなる傾向がある。ソフトローは改変が容易であり、可変性があるといえる。法令の解釈を少しずつ変えていく上での柔軟性もある。また、中間団体のソフトロー（ガイドライン）は、団体毎に異なっていても良いので多様性がある。新しい社会現象に迅速に対応できるので、予防機能がある。新規性と言える。悪法を少しずつ死文化させていく場合には、改革的といえる。

医師法21条（1906年）は、「医師は死体に異状があると認めたときには、警察に届け出なければならない」とし、刑罰を付している。長い間第三者の犯罪であるときは届け、医療過誤は届け出されない確立した習慣があった。しかし、医

療過誤が多発し、カルテ偽造も行われたにもかかわらず、民事裁判での患者の救済は進まなかった。1999年、優良な都立病院で、手術時の点滴液の薬剤に消毒液を入れるミスで患者が死亡し、最高裁は、死文化していた21条に違反したとして有罪とした。その後、医師が医療過誤を理由に起訴される例が増加した。私は、医師会と学会が作る第三者機関に届け出る義務を新設し、結果を公表するとのソフトローを作り、再度21条を死文化させることを提案している。
(b)
ドイツやアメリカでは、医療の場に警察が介入することはない。ましてや、故意の場合を除き、医療過誤で医師が刑事罰に問われることはない。医師会は、強い自治と民主的手続きに基づいて、患者のために強いソフトローを運用しているからである。米国医師会の規定では、「医療倫理が法に優先する」とされている。すばらしい規定である。米国やドイツの医師会は、私が提案した第三者機関などを含めて、自主的に医療の改善に取り組んでいる。
(37)

太田勝造教授は「法と正義の乖離やずれが大きく明白となっている」と言う。そこで、ソフトローの社会適合機能とは、法を正義に近づける努力を指す。古い法を時代の正義、地域の正義、集団の正義により合わせるべきだからである。
(38)

3. 自己統治と自治

ソフトローは、正義、善、憲法上の価値を実現するもので

第5章 自主規律（自己統治）

なければならない。その内容とプロセスはどのようなものか。以下の考え方と全く共通するものといえる。

　松井茂記教授は、政府権力の正当化について、現代福祉国家型リベラリズムでは、集団（結社）を結成し、政治参加する市民を前提とし、政治参加へのプロセスの保障の上で、利害関係の異なる集団の提携により、ある時点での政治共同体の決定がなされることを内容とするプリュラリズムによるべきと主張する。党派や団体が私益のみを求め、公益や諸権利を侵害することを阻止するプロセスを用意しなければならないとされる。[39]

　サンデル教授は「公民的美徳」の形成を多くの中間団体を含むコミュニティに求めている。すなわち、「多数決主義」、最大多数の最大幸福をめざす「功利主義」、「少数者の権利保護主義」、自由主義的福祉国家をめざす「リベラリズム」、ネオリベラルといわれる「リバタリアニズム」などを比較検討したうえで、リバタリアニズムが主張する完全に独立した個人の世界では市民はバラバラになってしまうし、リベラリズムでは個人は国家に依存し過ぎるようになり主体性がなくなるとして、多数決主義、功利主義、権利保護主義を尊重しつつ、多くの各種コミュニティを軸とする多元的かつ主権分散的な共和主義を唱えている。そこでは、「自己統治（self-goverment）」「自治（self-rule）」の確立も可能になるとされ[40]

ている。その結果、「公民性と共同性」が確保できることになり、コミュニティの中でも決して1回の多数決によるだけではなく、熟議することにより (deliberatively)、各人の利益、権利、平等が調整され正義が形成されていくとしている。

　私は、本書では、行政ソフトロー、公益団体ソフトローは、公益を目的にすることを前提としている。また、企業や諸団体といえども、今や市民、消費者、労働者の利益を考慮しない限り、マスコミ、ソーシャルネットワークなどの評価を得られない。過度の私益追求は、法令やソフトロー違反となり、社会的非難を浴び、損害賠償請求を受け、刑事罰を受ける結果となることがある。日本では、ソフトローを憲法上の規範として扱うべきこと、かつこれを熟議しながら柔軟に運用すべきことを強調したい。

II　民間ソフトローの法的効力（法的拘束力）

1. 民間ソフトローの正当性
(1) 実体的正当性

　ソフトローは憲法の定める価値、すなわち基本的人権や社会権を侵害してはならない。諸権利を侵害するソフトローは原則として無効である。日本では古いもの、不合理なものなど無効なものが多数あるので、団体内部で変えていかなけれ

ばならない。

(2) 手続的正当性

中間団体において、正当な手続きを経て成立するソフトローが手続的正当性をもつ。つまり、正確な情報が出される程、審議される時間が長い程、また、多数決を繰り返す程、正当性が高まる。

2. 拘束力の強弱

公的ソフトローの拘束力は一般的には強い。税務通達に違反する時には刑罰に該当することが多い。民間ソフトローの拘束力は、一般的には公的ソフトローに比べ弱い。しかし、拘束力がないと説明されていることはミスリーディングである。例えば、治療ガイドラインは、患者が病院に対して医療過誤を理由とする民事損害賠償請求の基準となるので効力はある。
(41)

3. 制裁方法（有効なもの）

民間ソフトローが手続的正当性と実体的正当性を有する時には、有効なものとして以下の制裁方法があり、その基準として充分に機能している。

(1) 公益団体の作る消費者や患者を守る安全規制のソフトローは、損害賠償請求の基準となる。

(2) 上記 (1) は、差止請求の基準ともなる。

(3) 団体において会員が規則に違反したときには、資格停止・

除名の基準となる。
(4) 違反者についての公表の基準となる（インターネットによるので効果は大きい）。

4. 司法審査（無効の場合）

ソフトローの無効を理由に、以下の請求訴訟をできる。
(1) 団体に対してソフトロー自体の無効確認訴訟と差止請求訴訟
(2) 団体やその役員に対する損害賠償請求訴訟
(3) 団体における資格停止・除名の無効確認訴訟（裁量権濫用）

民間ソフトローが憲法上の自由と権利を侵害する場合であっても、裁判所は無効として上記 (1) (2) (3) を認めることはほとんどない。団体の多数決という手続さえ整っていれば、団体自治を尊重する「部分社会の法理」を下に実体的正当性の検討に入らないからである。すなわち、ほとんど唯一の例外として、1996 年、最高裁により、高校においてエホバの証人の絶対平和主義の教義に基づく剣道実技への不参加を理由とする退学処分は、「社会観念上著しく妥当を欠き、校長の裁量権の濫用であり無効」とされた。

日本の後進性を示す最も重要な例は、2004 年、大谷医師が着床前診断を実施し、日本産科婦人科学会を除名されたことである。裁判所は除名無効と地位確認の請求、患者の損害

賠償請求のいずれも認めなかった。着床前診断は、英米では
(E)(g)
1990年より始まり、全世界に広まった。ドイツでは、医師
(h)
会が法律（刑罰）の禁止について、反対声明（ソフトロー）
を出し、2010年、着床前診断を実施した医師は無罪となっ
た。日本産科婦人科学会は、裁判では勝ったが、報道や世論
(F)
に負け、同氏の再入会を認め、２００６年構造異常の着床前
診断を認め、本年から、PGS（着床前診断スクリーニング）
の是非の検討に入った。
(k)

Ⅲ 安全規制と消費者保護

1. 規制改革

(1) 参入規制

　日本では長い間、各産業分野で、行政の許認可、業界団体
の加盟拒否による参入規制が広く行われてきた。独占禁止法
は長い間機能していなかった。最近になり、規制改革の立法、
または公正取引委員会の排除命令などにより、いくらか参入
規制が緩やかになりつつある。

(2) カルテル

　カルテルについては2006年にリーニエンシー制度ができ、
漸く効率化してきた。公正取引委員会が課徴金を課するケー
ようや
スはいくらか増加しているが、未だ少数に止まっている。

(3) 安全規制

　各団体における協議、協約により、安全の目的と称して、参入規制やカルテルが行われてきた。各団体は、長い間の慣行により変更できない状況にある。よって、各団体の役割は、消費者保護のための安全規制を目的とすることであり、今後は、より明確にすべきである。

(4) 司法審査

　独占禁止法及び、行政ソフトロー違反の取引妨害に対して、裁判所は差し止め請求、損害賠償請求をほとんど認めてこなかった。地方裁判所は、2011年に初めて、正面から独禁法１９条違反としてコンビニ本部の加盟店に対する拘束条件付取引による損害賠償請求を認め、またドライアイスの不当な取引妨害に対して、独禁法24条の差し止め請求を認めた。
(G)　　　　　　　　　　　　　　　　　　　　　　　　(H)

2. 消費者裁判手続特例法

(1) 消費者の直接請求

日本ではクラスアクション、三倍賠償制度がないために、消費者の直接請求訴訟は少なく、損害回収額も低くなっている。

(2) 団体による請求

消費者裁判手続特例法(2013年成立、3年以内施行)により、特定適格消費者団体が多数の被害者の代わりに請求できるようになったが、人身損害、拡大損害、逸失利益、慰謝料などの損害賠償請求を除外するとの大きな例外が作られてしまった。

第6章
社会国家における財政の課題

I 財政支出

1. 財政収支

　明治時代の国有企業の設立に始まり、社会主義と軍国主義の影響、戦後の傾斜生産方式により財政支出は極めて大きかった。福祉国家として、社会保障費が増大した。ケインズ経済学のスペンディングポリシー、需要喚起のための財政支出が拡大を続けた。

　2014年度政府予算の概要は、以下の通りである。

(1) 歳入　96兆円―税収50兆円、国債発行の借金４１兆円、その他5兆円

(2) 歳出　96兆円―公共事業費6兆円、社会保障費31兆円、教育費5兆円、国防費5兆円、国債返済23兆円

(3) プライマリーバランス（基礎的財政収支）

　　　(96 − 41) − (96 − 23) = − 18　18兆円の赤字

(4) 公債その他の借金　約1000兆円

(5) 消費税　1989年3%→1997年5%→2014年8%
→2015年10%予定（経済状況の好転を条件とする）

(6) 法的強制力　税金は極めて厳しく取り立てられており、年金の徴収も現在強化されつつある。反対に、歳出については、不正の受給がほとんど野放しにされており、取締りを強化できないので、実態すら明らかとなっていない。

第6章 社会国家における財政の課題

2. 公共事業費

　2009年の民主党政権において縮小したが、2012年の自民党復権で増加した。公共事業費を受ける側で、工事入札において既得権者の談合により、平等、公正が害されてきた。独占禁止法違反である。公正取引委員会により摘発されたのは一部でしかない。また、工事代金は元請業者から一次下請、二次下請、三次下請へ、さらに労働者にわたる。下請業者や労働者への配分は低くなる。2013年以降、放射能汚染の除染作業では、国や地方自治体から請け負った業者が、除染をしないで代金のみを取る詐欺的不正が横行した。

3. 社会保障費

　社会保障費は拡大を続け、教育費を含めると歳出の40％に至った。生活保護費、医療、介護、保育、失業対策などの極めて広い分野にわたる。補助金などの不正受給が横行している。生活保護費を虚偽の身体障害またはうつ病で取得すること、収入のある息子がいる母親が受給していたことが社会問題となった。2013年生活保護法の改正がされ、不正防止策をとった。他方で1957年から生活保護費の向上を目指す裁判が始まり、本年も集団訴訟が提起された。憲法25条は「健康で文化的な最低限度の生活」（生存権）を保障している。

　学説はプログラム規定説、具体的権利説、抽象的権利説がある。国会が生活保護法を定め、行政が具体的基準を定める

ので、最高裁は行政の裁量の範囲内として、請求を全て棄却している。地域や年齢などに分け、多くの人々が参加し、検討の上で具体的基準を定めるなど、ソフトローの特性を生かして運用すれば、人々の納得が得られるのである。

Ⅱ　不正受給対策

1. 財政支出の不正受給は広く行われ、かつ手口は秘かに巧妙である。これらを給付側の公務員が摘発することは極めて困難である。調査をする時間や労力をかけられないからである。また不正を見つければ、監督が充分でなかったという公務員自身の責任にもなる。一部でも返還されれば、刑事告発せず、また公表もしないことが多い。一般予防もできず、悪質な者は再犯を犯す。不正の手口は次々に伝播し、不正受給をしない者は損をするという風潮になる。これを防止するためには、密告制度と奨励金によるべきである。企業の不正行為や脱税などを取り締るには、内部告発という手段を使うことが効率的である。警察や行政庁の取締りには多大なコストがかかる。そこで、内部告発した者に利益を与えることにすれば、取締りを効率よく行うことができる。そればかりか、早期の発見により、大きな事件になることを未然に防ぐことも期待できる。

2. アメリカには良心的労働者保護法（Conscientious Employee Protection Act）があり、①報復措置の差止め、②被用者の地位の回復、③賃金等喪失の賠償（懲罰賠償も含む）、④使用者への罰金等を求めることができる。一方、日本では、これまで密告制度的なものはよくないとの意見も強かったが⁽⁴²⁾、2004年に公益通報者保護法ができ、2006年から施行されている。しかし、この法律はアメリカの制度を導入したにもかかわらず、企業自体が損害を受けないよう制限的なものになっている。アメリカでは違法行為がある場合のみならず、「それが起こる可能性が高いと合理的に信じられる場合」にも、告発した労働者は保護される。日本では法律の条文にここまで記載されていないが、条文を拡大解釈し、内部告発しやすいように法を運用しなければならない。

　また、アメリカの不正請求法（False Claim Act）は、連邦政府が企業や個人からの不正請求により損害を受けたとき、誰でも政府のためにその企業・個人に賠償請求でき、受領金の15～30％の報酬をもらえるようになっている。

III　情報公開制度

　日本では1980年代頃から、弁護士、ジャーナリスト、学者が中心となり、長期間の運動が行われた。欧米に遅れて、

1999年に、行政機関情報公開法が成立した。

政府と地方自治体では、情報公開室を設け、一定の開示がなされるようになった。しかし、防衛、外交などの開示制限は極めて厳しい。

また2003年に個人情報保護法の制定がされた。銀行からの借入者と患者の情報が開示されない状況があったので、情報取得は借入者と患者の権利であり、開示されるべきことを明記したものであった。しかし、社会では、個人の情報を原則として開示してはならないとの過剰な遵守が広がり、情報公開法の運用の拡大に制限がかかった。

また、2013年特定機密保護法の制定により、大きく制限されることとなった。これについては、日本弁護士連合会はツワネ原則によるべきものとの提案をしている。

情報公開法ではインカメラ審理の規定はないが、福岡高裁は、検証決定で事実上これを認めたが、最高裁は認めなかった。インカメラ審理を導入する改正法は、2012年廃案となった。
(1)
(43)

Ⅳ　医療保険制度

医療保険の運用は告示という行政ソフトローによっている。多くの問題があるが、直近の2つの例を挙げる。

第6章　社会国家における財政の課題

1. 同一建物居住者対象の報酬減額について

　老人介護施設が訪問診療医師に患者紹介料を要求し、取得することが広がり、保険医療の目的を害するので、厚生労働省はこれを防止するため、突然の措置をとった。すなわち、2016年4月に、同一建物居住者（集合住宅）における在宅時医学総合管理料（月に2回以上の継続訪問診療につき、月1回算定する報酬）を、自宅に対して約4分の1に減額改定し、訪問診療料を自宅に対して現行の約4分の1から半分（約8分の1）に減額改定した。

　すべての規範には一貫性・確実性・明確性・平等性及び予測可能性という特質が存するが、これらの特質を大きく害するのみならず、特に理由なく、予測可能性を大きく崩すものである。

　よって、当然ながら医療以外の分野では、このような予測可能性を破る理論も無く、実務も存在しない。例えば、賃金においては長い間不利益変更禁止の原則が理論及び実務において貫徹してきたところ、デフレ状況下に至ってもなお、3％又は5％など、段階的に減額をすることが例外的に認められているにすぎない。また、家賃減額においても、調停裁判の実務では、5％又は1割を限度とし、段階的に下げる方法を採っているのである。生活保護費や年金の決定も物価連動が

81

主たる争点にすぎない。

　すなわち、近年政府は医療関係者の反対にも関わらず、訪問診療の診療報酬を新設、付加することにより、大々的に訪問診療を政策誘導してきた。これにより、自宅でも集合施設でも十分かつ平等に医療を受けられる体制となりつつある。しかし、医師側から見れば、集合住宅における診察の労力が自宅における診察の労力の4分の1であるとは到底言えないと指摘されており、今回の大改定を許せば、集合施設での診療は著しく抑制されることとなる。その場合には、歩くこともままならず緊急的な医療を必要とする患者が、集合施設にいるというだけで医療を放棄・断念することとならざるをえない。

　これはまさしく、自宅にいる患者に対する集合施設の患者との差別的扱いとなるに他ならず、平等性を著しく欠くことは明らかである。そして、地域包括ケアを指導・誘導してきた従来からの政府の方針にも正面から反することとなり、一貫性を欠く。さらには、国民全体にとっての医療そのものに対する予測可能性をも大きく崩すこととなり、国民の医療への信頼が脅かされることとなる。

2. 訪問診療の16km制限について

　従来から、保険医療機関の所在地と患者の所在地との距離が16kmを越える往診については、明らかな無医地域である

第6章　社会国家における財政の課題

として厚生労働大臣の指定を受けた1号地域及び2号地域でなければ、原則として保険適用に基づく診療報酬請求を認めない扱いがされている。しかし、この16km制限は、安全規制の名の下に他地区への参入規制を目的としている。非常に古くからあるルールであり、現状に対応しなくなっており、まったく不合理である。1号地域及び2号地域の指定も、交通が発達した現代の日本において、指定要件を満たす地域はもはや存在しない。

　よって、16km制限に代わる新たなソフトローが必要であり、具体的には地域における多様性を認めるべきである。都市、山村などで分けて考えるべきである。予見可能性は重要である一方、ソフトローの運用は、人々の生活の利益のためには、また法の改革へ向けた試行のために、柔軟でなければならない。16km制限を行った結果、特に地方や離島においては患者にとっての不利益にしかならないことが明らかとなった以上、例外を設け、緩やかに運用すべきである。すなわち、地方において患者にとっての必要性が高い場合には、16kmを越えることを容認する、また、仮に必要性がなく16kmを越えたとしても、その部分のみの診療報酬の返還を行えば足りるはずである。しかし、他の報酬返還の例と同じに、診療した患者すべての報酬を返還させるという措置がとられる恐れが現に出てきている。この措置を許せば、患者のために採算

など顧みず懸命に尽くしている医師が、遠方にいる患者の在宅医療によっては保険収入を得られなくなり、患者救済を目的とする医業を継続できなくなることは一目瞭然である。この措置が違法で妥当でないことは明らかである。

　16km制限は、不合理な制限でもあるため、長い間、緩やかに運用されてきた。しかし、都市部では交通手段の発展により、短時間で遠くの集合施設へ行けるようになったため、上記1の措置と共に、この規制を強化する動きがある。しかし、地方や離島医療については全く状況が異なるのであり、現場、地域に合わせたソフトローの運用が必須といえる。

第7章
参政権と政党

I　二大政党から多数政党へ

　日本国憲法を含む近代憲法では、結社の自由を保障し、政党の役割を重視している。政党の網領（目的規定）、運営規則、決議事項などはソフトローとして法的効力を有する。最近では、党員への戒告、資格停止、除名が行われている。政党の定めたソフトローの手続に実質的に違反していなければ、裁判所は裁量権の範囲内として有効とするので、党員は訴訟をして争うことをしていない。そのために、日本では米国に比べ党議拘束が強すぎるとの批判がある。

　日本では戦前より政党政治が発展し、1995年には、政党助成法により議員数に応じて助成金が交付されている。中選挙区における複数当選、比例代表制としていた制度から、二大政党政治に誘導するために、1994年に主として小選挙区における1人当選制にした。長い間政権についた保守の党（現在の自由民主党）は、一度野党になった。また、2009年には民主党が衆議院で過半数をとったものの、参議院で自民党の過半数が続いていたため、いわゆる"ねじれ現象"が起こり、2012年の解散、総選挙により、自民党が衆参で過半数をとった。現在、その他は民主党を含め、少数政党が乱立する状況となってしまった。
(i)

　日本では二大政党政治は失敗し、将来は英国やドイツと同

じように三つないし四つの多数政党制、連立政権を目指すべきことが明らかとなってきた。その理由は、民意は多様であり、多くのソフトローは多角的に検討され改善されるべきだからである。多くの課題について各政党がこれらを各団体、行政、地方議会、国会へとつないでいく必要があるからといえる。そのためには、比例代表制、大中の選挙区における多数政党制が妥当といえる。

II 低い選挙率と死票

日本は経済大国、教育大国であるにもかかわらず、国政選挙での投票率は低い。10年前までは70％台、その後は60％台となった。地方議会ではほとんど50％以下である。積極的投票拒否とアパシーが含まれる。特に小選挙制になってから、少数政党に投票しても結果として死票となってしまうために、投票する意味がないと思う人が増加した。民意を反映し、多様なソフトローを形成していくためには、死票をなくし、比例代表とすることが必要である。

III 一票の格差（憲法違反）

日本では、以前より弁護士自身が原告となり、衆議院、参

議院における一票の格差が大きいことは憲法違反であるとの訴訟が申立された。多くの弁護士が参加し、最近「違憲」「違憲状態」との判決が多く出された。2013年、最高裁は「違憲状態」とした。日本では法令が憲法違反とされるのは極めて少ない。日本では人権侵害、差別が長い間続いてきたが、裁判所は「公共の福祉」により権利を制限できるとの理由から、被害者の救済をしなかった。しかし、一票の格差は庶民にも極めて分かりやすい問題であったため、地裁、高裁では多くの違憲判決も出された。

　但し、最高裁は直ちに実施された選挙を無効とするものではなく、予告的な意味を持つ「違憲状態」とする保守的立場に立ち、2013年に統一して終了させた。しかし、この問題は選挙区の区割を変えることで解決できる簡単な技術的課題に過ぎない。改革をできない日本人を象徴する課題として重要と言える。

Ⅳ　公務員制度改革

　政府には、東京の本庁と各県の支所がある。政権や大臣が変わっても公務員は変更されない。県、市、町にも同じように公務員が存在する。身分保障があるので、定年まで働く。政党、民間団体、市民が公務員とどのように協力できるか、

第7章　参政権と政党

公務員はそれらの意見をどのように扱うべきかが現在の大きな課題となっている。日本では公務員は戦後に成立した多くの行政規制を運用してきた。規制撤廃、規制改革の審議会の意見について、公務員は既得権益を持つ集団と結びついて反対を続けた。小泉純一郎首相は政治主導で規制改革と公務員制度改革に乗り出し、民主党政権でも進めようとしたが、公務員の強い抵抗にあった。現在の自民党政権も金融緩和、財政出動の実施に続いて経済成長（規制改革）の着手をすると言いながら具体化できない。公務員制度改革をしない限り、規制改革をできない状況である。改革のためには以下の二つの方策がある。

(1) 民間との人事交流

　全公務員の20～30％を、5～10年民間に出向させ、逆に民間人を行政庁に出向させる。民間人の生活、市場の動向を行政に反映でき、行政の改革も可能となる。

(2) ソフトロー改革

　行政のソフトロー改変は、民間からのボトムアップ、政党を介した政策提言によることができる。また民間におけるソフトローも、行政の適正かつ公正な政策を前提に、行政と協議できるプロセスの中で形成されることが理想的といえる。このようなソフトロー改革を通じて、規制改革への立法案が具体化できるものといえる。

第 8 章
3.11 大震災の放射能被害

I　帰宅困難地区

　1995年の阪神淡路大震災の復興は、地元の民意の形成（ソフトロー）と新しい法律により約10年で成就した。3.11大震災の大津波の被害からの復興も、阪神淡路大震災に学んで、次第に進みつつある。しかし、福島第1原子力発電事故の放射能被害を受けた地区についての復興は、日本では広島、長崎を除くと、歴史上初めての経験であり、極めて困難となっている。国費により放射能除染作業が行われているが進展していない。国や自治体は、当初は全員を帰宅させる方針であった。しかし、現在では帰宅を希望する者のグループ、帰宅せず他の地域に移転する者、現在決定できない者と、分けざるを得ない状況となってきた。概ね、3つのグループの中の民意について、ソフトローを形成する必要がある。その検討の中から、支援策、賠償額を決めていくこととなるが、進展しない状況となっている。

II　放射能身体許容レベル

　一般人の身体に対する許容レベルは、年間1mmシーベルトである。政府は当初、5mmシーベルトとした。最近では文科省が学校でのレベルの指針として、また原子力規制委員

会が帰還条件の指針として、20mmシーベルトを公表した。強い批判を浴びている。人々は自分の入っている学校、コミュニティー、団体で検討し、各組織のソフトローをもって運用するべきである。多様な方法で試行して、また改変して、より適切な基準を作るべきである。強制力を付与する必要があれば、法案を作ることとなる。ボトムアップによる手続でできる立法であるから、同時に運用ルールもあるので、円滑に運用されることとする。

Ⅲ 原子力発電廃止政策

1.国民の間では、原子力発電を廃止すべきとの意見が広まっている。特に、黒川清教授を委員長とする国会事故調の「事故は人災」とする報告書は、内外に大きな影響を与えた。[45]
3.11以後、定期検査も含めて17カ所の原発全てが停止し、2014年1月現在、大飯原発のみが稼働している。国会と首相官邸には、毎週金曜日にデモが行われている。約5つの政党は原子力発電廃止を提言している。民主党政権は30年後の廃止を提示した。しかし、2013年自民党政権は原発再稼働を決定している。日本全国の多くの団体やコミュニティーが原発停止を提言したり、原発再稼働に非協力的な決定をし、ソフトローを形成すれば、原発廃止に向けた行動となる。

しかし、人々はその方法論を認識していないために、そのようなソフトローを形成するに至っていない。多くの地方自治体の議会が原発廃止の決議（声明）をし、最近になり、小泉純一郎元首相が核廃棄物の処分困難を理由に原発停止を主張し、大きな力となっている。

2. 3.11まで、住民原告は運転差止請求と設置許可処分無効確認の2件の訴訟の下級審で勝訴したが、いずれも上級審で敗訴し、その他約33の同様の訴訟は全て敗訴している。3.11後の新しい訴訟には特別な注目が集まっている。住民は、東京電力の役員に対して株主代表訴訟を提起し、かつ、業務上過失傷害罪で刑事告訴したが、不起訴とされたので、検察審査会へ起訴するよう申立てている。

第 9 章
法の創造と法のイノベーター

I 司法の劣位

1. 2割司法の時代

　徳川時代末期、明治時代にオランダ、イギリス、フランス、ドイツ、アメリカの順に各国の法と文化が日本に入った。陪審や参審のない裁判制度、強い権力をもつ検察制度ができ、弁護士は分離修習を受け、司法者の監督下にあった。多くの人権侵害が起こり、戦争反対者は多数殺害された。しかし、戦後GHQの指導により、人権保障規定を含む近代憲法が成立した。裁判官、検察官、弁護士は統一した司法試験と司法修習をうけ、形の上では公正、平等な資格制度が確立した。弁護士は自治権を獲得し、懲戒権（監督権）が司法省から弁護士会に移行し、強力な身分保障を得た。全国に多数の法学部（4年）ができたが、司法試験合格者は約500人という少数であった。

　政財官の癒着構造、護送船団方式の国家運営（規制行政）が形成された中で、裁判の役割は個人、中小企業の紛争解決に限定された。行政や大企業を相手とする裁判は勝訴できず、ほとんど発生しなかった。また、弁護士以外の準法曹、あるいは隣接法律専門職種（隣接士業と呼ぶ）を認めたため、裁判外業務は隣接士業が担った。弁護士は裁判業務に限定されることとなった。この狭い分野が2割司法と呼ばれた。

2. 日弁連の改革運動

戦後の急激な高度経済成長の中で、多くの労働災害、公害、PL、薬害などが発生した。共産党、社会党及びこれを支持した労働組合連合も被害者救済をなし得なかった。司法消極主義に加えて、法曹の数の少なさから2割司法といわれた通り、司法の解決能力は小さかった。日本弁護士連合会は、実質的な法の支配を進めるために、法曹一元（弁護士から裁判官に任官すること）、刑事と民事の陪審制度の導入などの運動を長期間にわたって行ったが、法務省の反対により実現しなかった。

II 司法改革

1. 司法改革審議会意見書

1990年頃から、マスコミ、財界から法曹増員の要求が高まってきた。法曹三者（最高裁、法務省、日弁連）も賛成しなかった。1999年に司法改革審議会が開始した。第二東京弁護士会では、私が委員長をしていた法曹養成委員会を中心に、米国ロースクールの調査を経て法曹一元、司法研修所廃止、研修弁護士制度を内容とするロースクール構想を公表した。これを受けて、2001年、司法改革審議会は「ロースクール設立」、「重罪事件の刑事裁判員制度」を中心とする意見書

を公表した。「法の支配」を高らかに謳い上げた総論は、特に法科大学院実現後10年にして、具体的に実質化したか問題となっている。

2. 隣接士業の恒久化の危機[(47)]

上記意見書では、弁護士増員までの約10年間、隣接士業の権限の拡大と増員を認めた。10年の司法改革により、弁護士と隣接士業はいずれも増加した。現在弁護士は約3万5千人であるが、隣接士業は以下の通り約18万5千人いる。規制行政の規制する側を補助する面が強く、下記の行政庁の監督をうける。

税理士　7万4千人　税務申告（国税庁）
司法書士　2万人　登記申請（法務省）
弁理士　1万人　特許・商標申請（文化庁）
社会保険労務士　3万7千人　労務管理・社会保険申請（厚労省）
行政書士　4万4千人　行政への許認可・届出申請（各県知事）

司法改革審議会は、弁護士増員と共に、暫定的な隣接士業の増員を認めたために、隣接士業の恒久化という重大な危機に落ち込んでいる。法科大学院または法曹のほとんど全てがこれについて議論を開始しない状況である。

Ⅲ　法科大学院改革

法科大学院開始から10年を経て改革すべき時期にきた。

1. 法曹像

現在の議論において、教育の目的とする法曹像は何かが問われている。法曹の役割は、「法（ハードロー、ソフトロー）を創造すること」、「法を社会に適合させること」、「法を正義に近づけること」である。法曹とは「法の改革者」、「法のイノベーター」である。従前の議論ではソフトローは全くといっていい程、対象とされてこなかった。しかし、法曹は、ハードロー、ソフトロー、その他の規範もすべて統一して把握し、正義に近づける努力をしなければならない。つまり、それらの区別は絶対的なものではなく、相対的なものである。法曹となる者は、個別の法令を学ぶのではなく、法の生成、変動、消滅の原理を学ぶべきである。[48]

2. 隣接士業の廃止

隣接士業は、狭い分野の法知識についての試験で資格が付与される。一般的に、または国際的には法曹ではない。よって、その役割は法令を守ることであり、法を検討したり、法を改革することを任務とはしていない。法の支配の拡大、特に応答的法への改革には、法曹が市民社会の全域に入っていく必要がある。特に行政ハードロー、民間ソフトローを改革して

いく必要がある。萩原金美博士は、隣接士業は、歴史的には、特に監督官庁の監督の元に、規制行政を担うことであったことを強調する。今や規制改革が社会の目的となっている時代に、その役割は終焉したと言える(49)。社会の変化と共に減少すれば良いので、新規資格付与を停止するべきと言える。もちろん、現在の隣接士業の方の資格は継続する。法科大学院の協会は、隣接士業の業務を法科大学院で全て教育し、弁護士への統合を計る役割を担う重大な責務を負っている。従前の隣接士業への教育機関であった法学部を廃止して、質と量において法科大学院の充実を計るべきである。

3. 研修弁護士と法曹一元

　法科大学院修了者は、司法試験合格の後に、司法研修所において、現行の実務を研修するが、終了試験（2回目試験）を合格をするために、現行実務を無批判に受け入れることとなる。批判的精神を伸ばすことができない。最高裁と検察庁は現行制度に忠実な者を採用する。そこで司法研修所を廃止し、弁護士独立開業の条件として、弁護士事務所の2年間研修を義務付ける研修弁護士制度の提案がされた。イギリス、カナダの制度の例があり、実現は容易である。弁護士事務所の研修後、継続して勤務することになるので、5～10年して裁判官、検察官になる。自動的に法曹一元が実現する。法曹一元は長い間提案されてきたが、法曹増員と研修弁護士制

度により初めて実現可能となる。

4. 法科大学院協議会の重大な役割

司法改革によっては、裁判所の改革、判決の改革はなし得なかった。しかし、協議会は法科大学院の教育の拡充により、隣接士業の廃止、司法研修所の廃止、そして次の項で述べるように最高裁判事の就任を実現する力を有する。各法科大学院をリードするソフトロー形成に期待する。

Ⅳ 最高裁判所の司法消極主義

1. 違憲立法審査権の不行使

米国は日本と同じ違憲立法審査権を持ち、ドイツと韓国は憲法裁判所を持つ。上記諸外国では、数百の違憲判決が出されている。日本では、法令違憲判決と適用違憲判決が各約10件に過ぎない。その内容も取り上げるに値しない程であり、社会的に重要なものではない。その中で、2013年、最高裁が「非摘出子の相続分を摘出子の1/2とする民法900条」を憲法違反としたことは評価できるが、これも、以前から下級審で多くの違憲判決が出ていたにも関わらず、長い間その権利を否定し、多くの国で訂正された後にようやく認められたものである。

憲法9条は「戦争の放棄」「軍備及び交戦権の否認」を規

定する。1973年に地裁が自衛隊法を憲法違反としたが、高裁と最高裁は、憲法違反とはしなかった。現在まで、最高裁は「統治の根幹に関わる高度な政治問題については、一見極めて明白に違憲と言えない限り、司法審査権は及ばない」(統治行為論)としている。すなわち地方裁判所を始め、全ての裁判所では違憲立法審査権(憲法81条)を持ち、「司法権の優位」と呼ばれているが、現在まで「立法権と行政権の優位」は明らかである。基本的人権の保障する憲法は、形だけのイデオロギーとして実質化されなかった。今後は最高裁が司法積極主義に1歩でも踏み出すことを期待する。

2. 最高裁判所裁判官の任命

憲法79条は「最高裁裁判官を内閣が任命する」と規定する。しかし、運用では最高裁が15名を出身別に決める。裁判官(6名)、検察官(2名)、行政官(2名)の保守派が2/3を占め、残りを弁護士(4名)、学者(1名)が占めるのみである。保守派は常に多数派であり、司法消極主義に立ち、形式的な法の支配に止まり、応答的法、司法積極主義に進まない最大の原因である。

ディビット・S・ローは、「日本の最高裁を解剖する」を出版し、「アメリカの研究者からみた日本の司法」を批判的に紹介した。結論として、司法官僚制の支配を断ち切るために、「3つの各小法廷に1人ずつ憲法学者ないしは公法学者を任

第9章　法の創造と法のイノベーター

命すること」、「法学者の組織あるいは法科大学院のコンソーシアムに候補者リストを作らせること」を提案している。ディビット・S・ローの分析と提案は、日本の法学者を始め、法の改革を望む多くの日本人に、判例変更やソフトローによる確実な改革が可能であること、応答的法への道への可能性があることを示唆している。

THE REFORM OF JAPANESE LAW VIA SOFT LAW DEMOCRACY

Naoya Endo

Contents

Introduction 3

Ch.1 – The 'Four Stage Pyramid Model of the Legal System' as an Ideal 21

Ch.2 – Reform of the Criminal Trial System 47

Ch.3 – Reform of the Civil Trial 61

Ch.4 – Administrative Rules (prevention) 71

Ch.5 – Self-Governing Rules 85

Ch.6 – Fiscal Spending in the Social State 101

Ch.7 – The Right to Vote and Political Parties 117

Ch.8 – Radiation Damage from the 3.11 Great Earthquake Disaster 125

Ch.9 – The Creation of Law and the Innovators of Law 131

Main References 145

Introduction

I . Overview

Creative legal reform aimed at responsive law and judicial activism are necessary in order to substantiate the rule of law in Japan. For this purpose, it is necessary to separate what has been called law to present into 'hard law' and 'soft law'. In particular, the reforms that must be referred to as 'soft law democracy' are the most pivotal. The pathway to hard law reform through soft law reform promotes the development of the rule of law from the bottom up.

For the operation of law, the 4-stage pyramid model makes clear the legal roles and functions of (in order of strength of legal force) criminal justice, civil justice, administration (prevention), and the private sector (self rules). Developments in autonomous law could be seen in Japan after the war; however, also observed was a stifling atmosphere with regression to repressive law centered on criminal sanctions, entrenchment of judicial passivism, the case law of the conservative theory of self control community, and other phenomena. In response, we must take fresh pathways to responsive law, with liberalized strengthening of the self regulations of the administration and private groups as well as the flexible operation of soft law.

As a result, law schools clearly have the most important role in shouldering reform education for such operations of law. Legal professional education entrusted with comprehensive legal reform should be expanded, and moreover cover education in the domain of related professionals (i.e., abolish the position of 'related professionals') and education in the domain of judicial training (i.e., abolish legal training centers, and establish a trainee lawyer system, and a system in which judges are selected from experienced lawyers and legal experts) in order to lead the legal society. If these activities are undertaken, it is clear that many legal scholar and teachers will need to participate at the highest level of practice.

Ⅱ. The 4-Stage Pyramid Model of Legal System as Responsive Law

In the age of recovery, high economic growth, bubble

economics, and population growth that followed World War II, Japan emulated the Western model, and carried out policies through the 'top-down method' of the one-party rule of the Liberal Democratic Party (LDP). However, the 1990s signaled an age characterized by a deflationary economy and low economic growth, and from 2005 a decrease in population. Japan had become a mature developed country in economic and cultural aspects. People's lifestyle and culture diversified, and globalization rapidly progressed. Science and technology underwent remarkable development, and business and investment innovated new techniques.

In the West, the pathway to becoming a developed country was continuously accompanied by significant legal reform. However, in Japan, despite experiencing the social change that took place in developed countries of the world, the responsiveness of law was consistently delayed and legal reform did not progress. It had become an age in which the bottom-up formation of law as seen in the West was necessary, but this was not achieved. In the areas of market economics and medicine, law should maintain the social system and prevent conflict and crime. However, over the past 20 years, Japan has depended on old legal regulations centralized on an undeveloped country model of criminal law oversight. As a result, entrepreneurs, bureaucrats, certified public accountants, lawyers, and doctors are being criminally punished, one after another. This is particularly the case in relation to arrests, which TV and weekly magazines broadcast excessively, making it seem like a theatre-styled spectacle that can be likened to Rome's Coliseum.

Work experience over a long period of time and research into Western legal theory has led me to believe there should be a 'reconstruction of the rule of law' that is centered on strengthening of the civil trial and on prevention by the administration and private sector, not on criminal punishment. The limits of such a system, even in conditions of a representative democracy, are becoming clear throughout the world. In such a situation, in order to make clear the roles of domains that are responsible for the operation of law, each of the four stages in the pyramid model should be strengthened to make clear the roles and domains of those who are responsible for the operation of the law (in order of strength of authority (legal binding force): criminal punishment (prosecution, police), civil action (lawyers, courts), administrative regulation, and self governing rules).

Introduction

The main parts of the idea for this book as considered from an international viewpoint were presented at the 16th World Congress of the International Society for Criminology (Kobe) [1]*. Later this year it will also be presented at the Congress of the Japanese Association of Sociology of Law and The Annual Meeting of Law and Society Association (Minneapolis) in May, and at the World Congress of the International Sociological Association (Research Committee on Sociology of Law) (Yokohama) in July. Furthermore, in October this year the World Congress of the International Bar Association will take place in Tokyo. This book was published for the purpose of these conferences. In addition, when the Japanese people gain an understanding of 'soft law democracy', which aims to realize responsive law, and the 4-stage pyramid model, it will become evident that we can greatly contribute to legal reform if everyone does their part at their place of activity.

III. The Substantialization of the Rule of Law

In 1978, Nonet and Selznick demonstrated the historical development of the 'rule of law' by classifying its development process from 'repressive law', which relies on criminal sanctions, to 'autonomous law' which centers on regulation by civil law, and then onto 'responsive law', which represents a strengthening in mutual cooperation between the administration and the private sector [2]. In modern developed countries, responsive law is the ideal, and a 'responsive law' society is developing in the West. However, while Japan is on the pathway to 'autonomous law', there are occasional setbacks that return Japan to 'repressive law', since the administration of civil justice does not function robustly in Japan. In other words, the 'rule of law' is hollowed out and made meaningless. In 2011, Tamahana summarized past ideas relating to the 'rule of law' and considered implementation of 'substantial rule of law' as important for realizing constitutionally guaranteed freedoms and human rights, as well as the values of democracy and the welfare state. This is contract to 'formalistic rule of law', which considers a bad law good so long as it is enacted by the parliament [3]. This book will demonstrate in what ways the legal system should be reformed based on above concepts and a detailed understanding of how the legal system actually functions.

Japan was a 'repressive law' state with a focus on rule by the power of criminal punishment from the Edo, Meiji, and Taishō periods until World War II. However, it developed into a modern constitutional state and a 'autonomous law' state under the command of the Allied Forces (America) following World War II by the formation of a democratic constitution that included guarantees for fundamental human rights, pacifism, judicial review, etc. During the Cold War however, suppression by criminal punishment against the socialist movement continued, and civil relief — for pollution, work-related accidents, consumer harm, and other matters — failed to make progress, and the executive did not take preventative measures. Essentially, 'formalistic rule of law' continued with ongoing establishment of laws by the parliament, but 'substantial rule of law' that would see lives, people, lifestyles, and rights actually protected by law did not advance. It is clear that this was because of bad laws that restricted fundamental human rights for reasons of public welfare, courts not handing down judgments finding human rights restrictions in the operation of law unconstitutional, and, not an exaggeration, the power of judicial review never being exercised. In other words, the law could not progress to the stage of 'responsive law' while keeping pace with social developments in the rapid economic growth of Japanese society.

Many serious cases of pollution and malicious acts causing consumer suffering were dealt with by post-hoc criminal punishment: this was especially the case in the pursuit of liability by police and prosecutors of people involved with companies on a massive scale in order to quell the great social chaos that occurred after the collapse of the economic bubble. Criminal sanctions and the like of doctors and nurses of a kind not seen in the West were introduced because of increases in medical malpractice and lack of progress in civil relief for patient-victims. In other words, these phenomena all showed a retreat to a 'repressive law' society. Moreover, many yakuza gangs that have existed throughout the country from the Edo period continue to have connections with the ruling class. In a sense, the rule of violence by the visible power and invisible gangs has continued.

Given this kind of situation, the Bar Association and researchers, journalists, political parties who have been

Introduction

arguing for the substantiation of the 'rule of law' have made various recommendations and fruitful efforts to realize responsive law, the situation remains difficult. That is, legal reform lags considerably behind America and the EU. The main cause for this is that Japanese citizens, including lawyers, only passively accept the law, and do not actively create law themselves. For the most part, the kind of law in 'the rule of law' is hard law (i.e., the law of parliament). Most hard law in Japan has been copied from hard law in the West; it is already passive for this reason. Researchers, bureaucrats, and political parties participation in the creation of hard law, but this does not exceed a fraction of those with pertinent knowledge; the general public is hardly involved at all. Furthermore, when a law is created, the administrative executive drafts notifications and guidelines, and private groups also draft guidelines in accordance with it. Yet citizens can only comply with these guidelines as government orders, without room for criticism. In Japan, Western law is enacted somewhat conservatively, and there is also a tendency for soft law to operate conservatively.

Given such a situation, scholars and the mass media have continued to explain that hard law has legal binding force, but that soft law (administrative and private guidelines) does not. Soft law itself has not been treated as a target for the substantiation of the 'rule of law'. In other words, as there is no need for citizens to follow something that is not legally binding, experts, for the most part, have not included soft law in their studies for a long time. However, citizens have no choice but to follow the soft law they come into contact with on a daily basis. Even when the active improvement of soft law to conform to the times is necessary, this cannot be done by an individual. Thus, it is said that rather than generally following decided rules, Japanese people do so excessively. This observation is supported by history: a direct appeal (petition to a ruler or dictator) could lead to petitioner's head being severed and exposed to public view in the Edo period, violation of a village custom or duty could result in someone being ostracized or bullied in the Meiji period, and violations of internal regulations in the business world could lead to banishment (suspension of trade) in the Showa period. Without distinction between hard law and soft law, citizens have been put in a situation in which they have to seriously uphold all laws, even bad ones. When e.g. taxation notifications constitute the basis of criminal punishment and violations of a association's rules result in expulsion, then citizen's beliefs that soft law has legal binding force are reinforced.

Private associative groups reforming soft law and collaborating with the administration to continue to change soft law results in extremely meaningful legal reforms. It has become clear that scholars were mistaken in saying that soft law does not have legal binding force and in neglecting the importance of soft law. Currently scholars of administrative law research the legal binding force of administrative rules in the West, and views to the effect that soft law has legal binding force continue to appear even in textbooks [4] [5]. From 2004, and for the first time in Japan, the University of Tokyo's 21st Century Center of Excellence run by Nobuhiro Nakayama and others analyzed soft law from various angles and published the results [6]. For five years I have continued to publish essays and books that have explicitly held soft law to have legal binding force [a][b][c][d]. The soft law that citizens interact with plays an important role: whereas hard law is abstract, soft law is the living law. When soft law contravenes the constitution or a law, then there is no need to follow it. Additionally, bad soft law should continue to change. The bottom-up method is desirable, in which the administration and private groups associations can make soft law, trial it, enact hard law, change it, and abolish it. Legal reform from soft law, i.e. what should be called 'soft law democracy', is the 'pathway to responsive law', and can be understood as the substantiation of the 'rule of law'.

In 1835, de Tocqueville saw the freedom of association and the self governing codes(soft law) of conduct of not just political parties but of civil groups as the most important elements of America's democracy [7]. In Japan, there is a history of groups being created under the leading power of the administration or for oligopolistic purposes; however, this must be fundamentally reformed. Until recently, associations and companies committed many scandals and were subjected to criticism by the mass media and to the police investigations. If associations and companies make robust soft law with voluntary imposition to put it on sound footing, they can reduce criminal cases and escape from 'repressive law' so that they can conform to social changes and aid the substantiation of the rule of law. Disclosure of information on the activities of the administration, associations, and companies, and the reflection of citizen opinions in accordance with social changes will demonstrate the development of the law. Furthermore, for unavoidable disputes, if 'autonomous laws' advance that settle the dispute at an early stage by civil justice, new policies will take off from the scene, and a smooth transition to 'responsive law' will become possible.

IV. Administrative Deregulation and Civil Justice Reform

In the contents of the Structural Impediments Initiative in the 1990s, America sought amelioration of the closed nature and exclusivity of the Japanese market. As a result, the Antimonopoly Act was strengthened, exclusions to the application of the Antimonopoly Act abolished, and administrative regulations relaxed or abolished. In addition, the Administrative Procedure Act (1993), the Act on Access to Information Held by Administrative Organs (1999), and the Act on the Protection of Personal Information (2003) were all established. In this way, laws promoting growth of the market economy, and laws for an information-oriented society providing for the administrative support of the private economy were put in place. Legislation for a free economy and a welfare state were achieved by following the West while being unable to reform the civil justice legal system.

In this book, I will identify the inadequacies of this 'hard law' system. However, even already-established hard law cannot operate proactively; this book takes as a theme the reforming of the thinking and behavioral patterns of Japanese people, who conservatively interpret and passively apply it. In other words, 'soft law' should be created to actively manage 'hard law', and new 'hard law' should be created via the enrichment of 'soft law'.

V . Haruki Murakami's '1Q84'

'1Q84', written by Nobel Prize candidate Japanese author Haruki Murakami, became an international bestseller and is highly esteemed as literature [8]. However, it is not from the viewpoint of literature, but the viewpoint of a lawyer that I want to highly appraised Murakami's unintentional yet wonderful description of the lag in Japan's 'rule of law'.

Introduction

The main character (a woman) murders offenders of domestic violence with a needle one after another in order to rescue female victims. The book also depicts situations in which the left-wing groups and religious cult groups seen in Japan commit crimes, which ultimately leads to their self-destruction; however, rescue by legal means is not expected at all.

Murakami does not signal trust or reliance on legal professionals, police, and other groups in the slightest. The fantasy targeting the 'rule of law' in its broad meaning, which includes NPOs and relief organizations, is completely discarded. I think that by depicting such a hyper-realistic world, it will likely be subject to negative appraisals by a realism-like literature perspective. It had the result of good religious salvation while criticizing bad cults. It affirmed good violence, and repudiated bad domestic violence. From the point of view of the historic continuation of the history of Japanese popular literature, this type of rewarding good and punishing evil is a big success. From the Edo period to today, good violence by good officials and good yakuza has been glorified and situations where violence has had to be used have been repeatedly depicted in novels and film, such as by Mito Komon, Ohoka Sabaki, Zatoichi, and Shimizu no Jirocho(yakuza). However, regardless as to whether it is an exercise of authority or self-salvation, resolution through this kind of violence is no more than an emergency countermeasure, not a medium- to long-term remedy. Consequently, even in Murakami's modern novel, there is the great sense of crisis that the 'rule of law' is being completely ignored, and that the public unconsciously express their agreement. In developed countries, the social system must be restored by people's opinions and actions, not by relying on violence. Interpersonal relationships, interchange, and the exchanging of opinions become important for this purpose. In Japan, insufficient heated debate and Socratic dialogue in relation to social problems must become more proactive.

I would like everyone to overcome, even just a little, the world in 1Q84, and with courage, face the reality of society so that democracy can progress. I publish this book in both Japanese and English, so to present to the Japanese people 'topics that must be resolved' and to have everyone overseas understand 'Japan's present situation' and the 'future in which we must advance'.

Chapter 1

The 'Four Stage Pyramid Model of the Legal System' as an Ideal

Part 1 – Advancement Towards Responsive Law (the Rule of Law in Substance)

1. Figure 1: Pyramid Model (Criminal Punishment → Civil Justice → Administrative Regulation → Self Governing Rules): the responsive law system

As the Introduction showed, the prevention of crimes and disputes should be conducted through various systemic policies, but with the caveat that criminal punishment as a post-facto sanction should be suppressed. Relief and sanctions of civil justice should be developed, and cooperation by the administration and the civil sector should take place for prevention. Thus, the ideal for Japan is the 4-stage pyramid model in Figure 1 (responsive law system). The reverse pyramid model in Figure 2 represents the situation until now, for which further reform is necessary to strive for the ideal model in Figure 1. The pyramid model represents, from top to bottom, a qualitative weakening in 'coercion, legal sanctions, and legal binding force', and a quantitative broadening of 'human resources, range of laws, and social functions' which every stage in the system is burdened by.

2. Figure 2: Reverse Pyramid Model (Administrative Regulation → Intermediary Groups → Criminal Punishment → Civil Justice): the formalistic law system

Until the 1990s, Japan prioritized industrial development driven by the state, and administrative prior regulation (permission and authorization) and strong administrative guidance took place, including collusive bidding at the initiative of government agencies. The Antimonopoly Act was not able to play its role sufficiently, and so every industry group and regional group in the country took on the role of carrying out administrative guidance. Non-compliance with the system meant failure for one's economic activities. This kind of system in which the freedom of speech had been suppressed gave rise to war, pollution, chemical hazards, and nuclear reactor accidents. The victims of these disasters were not able to receive sufficient relief through civil trials. Furthermore, the social role played by civil trials was extremely small, as it was rare for citizens and small- or

The 4-Stage Pyramid Model of the Legal System

Figure 1: The Responsive Law System

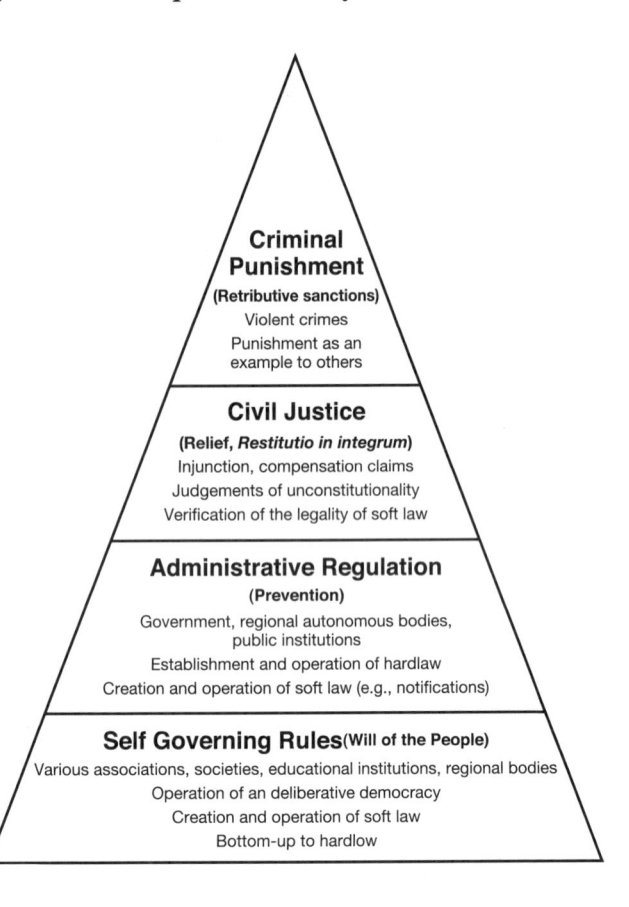

Criminal Punishment
(Retributive sanctions)
Violent crimes
Punishment as an example to others

Civil Justice
(Relief, *Restitutio in integrum*)
Injunction, compensation claims
Judgements of unconstitutionality
Verification of the legality of soft law

Administrative Regulation
(Prevention)
Government, regional autonomous bodies, public institutions
Establishment and operation of hardlaw
Creation and operation of soft law (e.g., notifications)

Self Governing Rules (Will of the People)
Various associations, societies, educational institutions, regional bodies
Operation of an deliberative democracy
Creation and operation of soft law
Bottom-up to hardlow

Figure 2: The Formalistic Law system

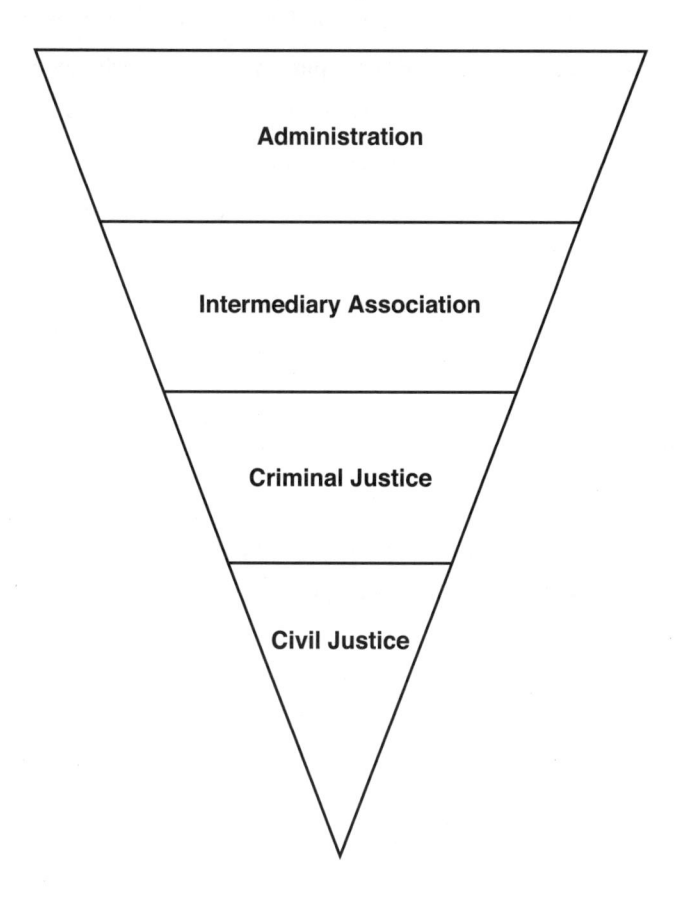

medium-sized companies to win against large companies or against the government.

In my previously published material, the model was 'administration → criminal punishment → civil justice → intermediary groups'. However, this has been revised as above. Professor Hayley and Professor Tatsuo Inoue completely endorse the view that 'Japan is a society ordered more by extralegal and often quite coercive community and group controls than law or government power.' [9] [10]. A system of repressive law in which freedoms and rights are violated is the consequence of relying on sanctions of administration, intermediary groups and criminal power. However, this is superficially referred to as the formal legal model because they were enacted after the war through the creation of laws and notifications.

3. Regulation Reform

In the 1990s, with influence from the West, a number of voices in favor of relaxing administrative regulations began to surface. In 2000, regulation reform was initiated by Prime Minister Koizumi Junichirō and Cabinet Minister Heizō

Takenaka (Liberal Democratic Party). Scholars and journalists explained that 'prior regulation becomes unfair and unequal' and that 'a good social system would make use of sanctions (criminal punishment) or relief (civil punishment) after a conflict or crime takes place'.

However, this explanation is inaccurate; the explanation below is correct.

(1) The primary purpose of the legal system is to prevent conflict and crime. There is a need for the administration, intermediary groups, and citizens to create the system and to constantly change it. Taking a policy of strict punishment and increasing the scope of what constitutes a crime does not result in prevention, and harms the system. It is also necessary to conduct civil actions to realize the purpose of public policy, as is done in America.

(2) The second aim is to aid victims through civil actions. The civil action system must be strengthened to be like that in America. For instance, taking asbestos victims as an example, early relief was conferred through litigation in America, and through administrative legislation in Europe. However, in Japan, relief was remarkably slow, made mostly through litigation, but also supplemented by administrative legislation.

(3) The third and final measure would be the sanctioning and segregation of criminals[p][q].

Part 2 – The Strengthening of the Role of Each Stage (Reform)

1. Criminal Punishment

In Japan, the target of enforcement has become excessively broad, ranging from insignificant crimes to market and medical crimes. This should be radically re-prioritized. Enforcement against violent crimes (murder, rape, etc.), abductions by North Korea, and the like should be strengthened. On the other hand, the authority of criminal punishment should not intervene in the areas of the market and medicine.

2. Civil Action

The discovery system is inadequate, and there are situations where it is not possible to elucidate the truth[r]. For this reason, there has been a tendency for compensation sums to become lower. Furthermore, relief for victims is not satisfied as the level of proof for victims seeking compensation is high probability[e]. It is necessary for the civil trial system to be strengthened in order to sanction the perpetrators, and not rely on the criminal law[d].

3. Administrative Power (Central&Local Government)

The preventative function of administrative power should be strengthened. Previously, bureaucrats (executive) colluded with politicians and businessmen in order to make strong regulations for economic growth. Abolishment of regulations and regulation reforms began in the 1990s. Conversely, preventative regulations for the safety of consumers, workers, and children should be strengthened.

4. Self Governing Rules(Associations)

In the past, associations and academy groups followed the instructions of administrative authority, in addition to creating soft law (collusion) to protect their interests.

However, henceforth self governing rules as soft law should be made to reflect the stand point of the citizens, consumers, and workers.

Part 3 – Specific Examples

1. Pursuing Responsibility for the Collapse of the Bubble Economy

The massive amounts of loan credit held by many banks became nonperforming loans as a result of the collapse of the bubble economy in 1990. Loan beneficiaries such as real estate agents who had borrowed using window-dressing settlements of accounts were criminally punished. This method was unavoidable. However, it was completely wrong to indict and criminally punish the acts of bank officials who granted loans anticipating that they would not become nonperforming loans, the acts of certified public accountants who could not see through the window-dressing, and the lawyers who were seen as evading compulsory procedures for participating in asset transfers for debtors. It is not necessarily possible to accurately predict large fluctuations in the economy. Criminal punishment for economic activity should be limited to clear intent, malicious fraud, and threats. Reform of the civil trial was important for making the litigation concerning credit collection of the banks more effective, faster, etc. Improvement of soft law for the improved operations of the civil trial process, rather than just reforming hard law, was important. However, these did not take place.

There were also no operations to treat nonperforming loans as taxable losses, nor was there repayment. In the case of certified public accounts and lawyers, it would have been sufficient that each their association they investigate to and give a warning as punishment. In the case of many banks, officials were criminally punished, mere sued derivative lawsuits brought against them, and lost lawsuits concerning massive amounts of damage. I advocated that the damage should be divided up among officials in the judgment and reduced[f]. In 2006, an upper limit for damage amounts was established through an amendment to the Commercial Code.

2. The Act on the Protection of Specially Designated Secrets

This Act passed in 2013. It overcame not only the objections of the opposition party, but also those of many journalists and citizens. The text of the Act was only made completely public seven days prior to the vote in the House of Representatives. There was no time for the Japanese people to debate it. The provisions of the text were abstract.

Just by establishing the 'legislation', the 'enforcement orders, which give it substance (cabinet order)', and 'the guidelines, which ease its operation' were not passed at the same time. It would be ideal for the operations of the law to be examined to the level of guidelines (i.e., its soft law) and passed simultaneously. The bill provided that the release of designated secrets would be examined within a 5-year period. Large conflicts in opinion would diminish if this decision period could be set to a week, a month, three months, six months, a year, etc. in these guidelines..

3. Compensation Claims of Leprosy Patients

A policy of strictly segregating patients in a facility was adopted in pre-war Japan. The policy of segregation did not change even when antibiotics were used to stop infection after the war, and the Leprosy Prevention Act was enacted in 1953. This law was abolished in 1996. Patients issued a state compensation claim in 1998, which they won in 2001. Guidelines for gradual release should have been made and implemented through the cooperation of patients, doctors, local residents, and facility administrators. It is not as if such efforts should not have taken place at all; it was because there were supporters that the law was abolished, and that the litigation was successful. However, there should have been a plan to consciously create soft law to overcome bad law, through which the movement could have nullified or repealed the law more quickly.

4. Assisted Reproductive Technology

Generally, laws, ethics, and morals lag behind as society changes. There are cases where, if engaged in an act that goes against laws or ethics, the consequence may be criminal punishment, a civil trial, or disciplinary action. Even a bad law is a law. There is a risk that even justifiable acts that respond to the appeals of society result in the above sanctions when done alone.

Doctor Kikuta was accused of the crime of creating a false document because he recorded the birth certificate of a child that a couple had adopted from a high school student as being the actual child of the couple, and his qualification as a Designated Doctor under the Eugenic Protection Act (Designated Doctor under the Maternal Health Protection Law) was revoked. Doctor Rihachi Iidzuka (professor at Keiō University) carried out artificial insemination with donor semen (AID) from 1949 and was criticized. In 1999, Doctor Nezu was struck off the Japan Society of Obstetrics and Gynecology for publicizing in vitro fertilization using the egg and sperm of donors. In the guidelines of the Japan Society of Obstetrics and Gynecology on in vitro fertilization, it had been stated that doctors must only carry out in vitro fertilization between couples. Doctor Ōtani was similarly expelled in 2004 when it was reported that he had conducted a preimplantation genetic diagnosis.

With the above three people I established 'From' (the conference supporting Fertility Right of Mothers) and publicized an operational policy (soft law) recognizing egg and sperm donors, host mother birthing, and preimplantation genetic diagnosis[g][h].

The Japan Society of Fertilization and Implantation and the Japan Society for Reproductive Medicine began to comprehend the situation, and by 2013 the Japan Society of Obstetrics and Gynecology too had begun applying the guidelines flexibily. We have now reached a stage in which a new law recognizing sperm and egg donors and host mother is being prepared[j].

Part 4 – Soft Law Democracy

1. Hard Law

The laws that the Diet of Japan (the House of Representatives and the Councilors) enacts and the ordinances that regional assemblies establish are hard law. In constitutionalism, which has representative democracy at its core, law is established by the assembly, which is endowed with supreme authority and validity. Accordingly, the procedures are strict, the legal binding force is strong, and modification is difficult. However, since the expressions of hard law are abstract, its specific interpretation and operation continues to change via soft law. As such, there is no need for short-term modification.

2. Soft Law

Soft law originally indicated international law and was considered the law that did not have the state's binding power. It had been considered weak and not to have legal binding force. However, in the development of the EU, the role played by soft law is incredibly large [11]. This book treats the following rules, which are established outside of the 'assembly', as soft law. Generally, rule (1) below is said to be hard law from its legal basis and the clearness of its binding force, and is not called soft law. However, I treat only administrative legislation for which modification is easy as soft law. Rules (2) and (3) are generally said not to have legal binding force, but it is acknowledged that they have various legal effects. There are times when contraventions of administrative soft law result in punishment, or violation of civil soft law give rise to expulsion or compensation claims. The foundations of its legal force include decisions by a majority vote in administrative organizations and civil groups, consensus, and organizational decisions, and are largely similar to the formation processes of hard law.

(1) statutory orders (set by the executive)

　　cabinet orders – enforcement orders set by the cabinet

　　ministerial orders – enforcement regulations set by each minister

(2) administrative rules (executive soft law), executive guidance

(3) civil sector soft law (the soft law of non-profit associations and civil groups)

3. The Limits of Representative Democracy

Parliamentary democracy, in which representatives are chosen through an election, is not direct democracy, but indirect democracy. While citizens can express their will at the time of the election, there is doubt as to whether political parties and parliamentarians can reflect the will of the citizens. It is also viewed as uncertain whether parliamentary democracy can protect people's lifestyle and welfare, or spur development of the economy. Furthermore, even if citizens desire reform of a specific item, citizens cannot directly construct laws. It is extremely difficult for people to make, modify, or abolish hard law. From the point of view of the citizens, hard law is something in the far distance. Citizens expect less and less from representative democracy, and there is a decreasing tendency in the number of people who go to vote.

Other kinds of democracies are being pursued [12].

4. Application of Soft Law (Bottom-up)

Civil sector soft law is something extremely close to citizens. It is something that is simple for citizens themselves to establish and modify. Administrative soft law is easier to modify than hard law. There is a mountain of old administrative soft law in Japan, and this constrains the freedom of economic activity. Up until around 15 years ago, it was difficult to modify something once it had been created. However, modification of administrative soft law has increased with the development of regulatory reform and transition of power to the Democratic Party of Japan (DPJ). The petition movements and signature-collecting campaigns by NPOs, NGOs, and intermediary groups have become numerous [13]. However, it is ideal to change administrative soft law while continuously running trials and experiments according to the framing of the soft law made by the intermediary groups themselves. Soft law democracy is this bottom-up progression of transitions from civil sector soft law, to administrative soft law, and then to hard law. In 2009, John Keane introduced the idea of 'monitoring democracy' in the modern world, with soft law as the most central of its pillars. This is because social networks, demonstrations, and the like are important as telecommunication methods, but it is not necessarily the case that they will rise to the norm of law [14].

5. The Characteristics and Functions of Soft Law

(1) Soft law has the following characteristics.
1. Flexibility (it can be interpreted smoothly to a certain degree)
2. Adjustability (it is responsive to a situation and can be changed easily; its procedures are simple)
3. Affirmativeness (its point is to decide a matter for the time being, meaning that measures are specially taken in response to a social situation)
4. Deversity(even soft law differing between regions and groups is acceptable)

(2) The following points are important from the point of view of making and altering soft law.

1. Information

Gathering information and disclosing it to interested parties

2. Discussion

Analyzing the above accurate, diverse information, and the interested parties discussing it

3. Publicization of new plan

Publicizing a new plan based on the above discussion and

seeking additional opinions

4. Implementation

Actually implementing the alteration or enactment based on the above new plan

5. Prior notification

Making an announcement to the mass media in advance, and conveying it to society. Furthermore, in circumstances that relate to criminal punishment, notifying the police

(3) The position of not following bad laws and trying to make good laws including soft law has the following benefits.

1. One can take the position of always examining whether a law is good or bad.
2. There is no gospel to protect as bestowed. Things that are decided from above are no longer accepted without questioning.
3. One can always consider whether there is a new way of doing something.
4. One can always debate whether a law is good or bad, and what the new law is.
5. Democratic procedures and the democratic system of organizations are preserved because free discussion

in civil sector groups and in government offices is guaranteed.

6. Accurate information is always gathered.
7. Information is always disclosed and transparency can be increased.
8. The ill effects of treating the governors as more important than the governed are removed.
9. It is a bottom-up method and can reflect the will of the citizens.
10. New measures that would be useful to bureaucrats and parliamentarians can be presented.
11. One becomes conscious of the fact that abolishing a bad law and making a good law is not only for one's own benefit, but also always for the public benefit.

6. Court Judgments

Japan doesn't have the constitution court like in German and Korea. From the point of view that judicial review by the Supreme Court can make a provision of law invalid as same as in U.S.A., court judgments exceed the strong binding nature of hard law. In relation to this:

Ch.1 – The 'Four Stage Pyramid Model of the Legal System' as an Ideal

(1) Up until the Supreme Court judgment is released, judicial review by district and high courts is multiform and affirmative. It is similar to soft law in this aspect.

(2) From the district courts to the Supreme Court, judgments are used for the interpretation of laws and the application of laws. In each judgment, there are the soft law characteristics of flexibility, multiformity, and affirmation. From the point of view that the interpretations of laws should conform to social change and the applications of laws should be proactive and align with a purpose, judgments should be thought of as similar to the operations of soft law.

(3) In 2014, the famous judge and researcher Hiroshi Segi published his book 'The Hopelessness of the Courts' (Zetsubō no saibansho) after retiring as a judge. In it, he argues: 'Japanese courts are ruled by the Supreme Court Secretariat, a situation extremely similar to a Soviet-style totalitarian, communist system. Judges have no independence, something that is supposed to be constitutionally guaranteed. Rather than handing down verdicts that protect human rights and

justice, they predetermine conservative conclusions whose reasoning is almost entirely formalistic....We must abolish this system of bureaucratic judges and introduce one in which judges are chosen from a pool of lawyers' [15].

In a survey conducted in 2000 among people who made use of civil courts, only 18.6% answered that they were satisfied with the litigation system, and only 22.4% answered that it is easy to use [16].

To change this situation, the whole nation, including experts, must understand how important the application of the law is and improve it little by little. In Japan, there has been too much adherence to precedent in judgments. This must continue to change flexibly, in the same way as soft law does.

(4) In 2013, Ryō Kuroki wrote the novel The Kingdom of a Judge's Robe (Hōfuku no ōkoku) based on accurate research. In this novel, which should be classified as nonfiction, Ryō Kuroki depicts a situation in which the Supreme Court Secretariat uses unjust job relocation and reassignment and continues to damage the independence of the judges, as well as a situation in which many anti-nuclear reactor lawsuits

are lost by plaintift residents [17]. Together with Hiroshi Segi's report (above) it can be said that at the time of the 2-year Judicial Reform Council judges became somewhat activist, but went straight back to repressive law in the courts.

Chapter 2

Reform of the Criminal Trial System

Part 1 – Prioritization and Alternative Proposals

1. Violent Crimes

From before the war until around the 1970s, the main object of police and prosecution oversight was the socialism movement (workers, students). Following this, prosecution oversight began to intervene in all kinds of citizen activities. Despite this, the object did not reach the point of cracking down on violent crimes, especially the elimination of organized crime groups. Even oversight provided by the Anti-Organized Crime Law (1991) was insufficient, and so it was further strengthened in all prefectures in 2012 by the Ordinance for Eliminating Organized Crime Groups. As a result of this Ordinance, the obligation to cease relations between organized crime members and close connections is placed on the citizens, though it is not yet similar to anti-organized crime legislation in other countries. A countless number of violent crimes have taken place, as exemplified by abductions by North Korea, the mass murder by Aum religion group, killings by stalkers, and the like. It is said that there are around 600 unsolved cases.

Even after the war, around 10 cases of retrial decisions for false convictions have been made, including those in which facts had only come to light following 20-40 years of imprisonment. Consequently, confidence in the judiciary has been shocked. It is clear that costs and members of the police should be transferred to violent crime.

2. Excessive Intervention in the Market and Medicine

From the 1970s, the object of police oversight increased to cover cases of large-scale fraud and corrupt business practices, pollution, economic crimes, and the like [18]. In 1990, the collapse of the bubble economy began, and the subsequent deflation economy has continued to the present day. Excessive bank loans became enormous nonperforming loans. Bank executives were arrested one after another, and were found guilty. Furthermore, cases of stock exchange-listed companies using fraudulent accounts arose, and officials and certified public accountants were criminally punished for the crime of making false security statements. Furthermore, doctors were arrested and found guilty for committing medical malpractice. In this way, entrepreneurs, certified public accountants, lawyers, doctors, and nurses were arrested and found guilty.

However, the people found guilty were engaging in general business activities, and from a subjective or objective viewpoint, it cannot be said that they were criminals. Of course, it would have been possible to prosecute the most egregious offenders in order to make the punishment of the crime an example for others. However, by prosecuting people who were not malicious, some were eventually found innocent and social unrest increasingly fomented. In the same way, the people found guilty were only a small portion of the many people who had contravened the same law.

The prevention and resolution of these problems should not rely on criminal punishment they should be achieved by other methods. Prevention and resolution should be done by civil trial or through a group's self rules. According to research into social dilemmas, the smaller the group the better the communication is and the more cooperative action can be taken [19]. The mutual promotion of cooperative action is seen as important [20]. For this reason, the creation of soft law should begin in small regional and organizational groups.

3. Countermeasures for Corporate Crimes through Soft Law

Breaking up companies and groups via criminal punishment is necessary when targeting ill-natured corporate crimes and business crimes involving violent groups. On the other hand, as for general companies, the laws protecting consumers, investors, and workers, and laws protecting the environment and sanitation can be adhered to by putting into place an environment (situation) of preventative measures that include surveillance though methods of environmental criminology. Criminal punishment is not relied on; there is a need to combine various methods [21].

The 'enforced self-regulation' suggested by the criminologist J. Braithwaite is slightly similar to Japanese employment rules: companies make rules that conform to a fixed situation, and these are implemented and subjected to surveillance on the agreement of the regulatory authorities. J. Braithwaite demonstrates various alternative proposals in the form of responsive regulation and also identifies post-facto restorative justice that does not operate through criminal punishment [22].

Furthermore, in America a system in which prevention and reductions in criminal punishment has progressed in line with federal guidelines (1991) for assessing the culpability of organizational bodies through the creation and implementation of internal company compliance programs[23]. In Japan too, manuals for internal controls and preventing power and sexual harassment have been put into place [24]. The above are both instances of companies internally creating sensible soft law voluntarily. This is a necessary method in order to avoid criminal punishment.

Furthermore, the effectiveness of such a system is low even if an individual in a company is criminally punished. As a system for reforming the company itself when there is an illegal act by an official of the company, there are important provisions in the Financial Instruments and Exchange Law and Medical Care Law that allow governmental agencies to dismiss (and recommend) officials. When there are no such provisions via law, a method of regulation articulated in the company or group's statutes can be said to be effective.

4. Rectification of Benefit Administration

In the welfare state, massive amounts are being paid out for social security, and there is an increasing amount of people receiving welfare fraudulently. Unjust receipt of money is prevalent even in cases of financial expenditure for economic stimulus measures such as public works projects. It is impossible to crack down on all of this through criminal law. Benefit administration should be made more fair and efficient by utilizing internal report systems, etc.

Part 2 – The Underdevelopment of Criminal Practice (Restraint) (Reforms of Four Shortcomings)

1. Expansion of Bail (Dissolution of Hostage Justice)

The intent of Article 89 of the Criminal Procedure Act is that a suspect must be released on bail when there is no risk of escape or that evidence may be concealed. It is not written in the text that bail can be set when a confession has been made, nor is it written that bail cannot be set when there is no confession. Nevertheless, in cases where there is no confession, custody following arrest can be around 23 days, and can reach up to 2 or 3 months when custody following indictment is included. Custody continues even after the first public trial in some cases where the suspect does not confess. The established practices of bail are completely in a state of illegality. Hostage justice is operations by which police or prosecution have restrained an individual, they coerce a confession, and set bail once there is a confession. Henceforth, the Bar Association and the courts should deliberate over improving the operations of bail, so that bail is permitted even when there is a denial directly following indictment. A bail system throughout the period of custody from three days after the arrest should be legislated.

2. Shining a Light on Interrogation (Overemphasis of the Confession Record)

In Japan, since the Edo period, the confession had been regarded as 'the king of evidence'. Prior to World War II torture had become something normal, and even following the war interrogation by violence and also mental abuse continued. Confessions were obtained through interrogation over a long period and by threatening to arrest family members and other relations. Tape recorder recordings have not been conducted, even to the present day. There have been strong criticisms of the criminal investigation process arising from an evidence forgery case by public prosecutors in 2010 (wherein three public prosecutors were arrested and prosecuted). An examination into making interrogations more visible has begun.

3. Realization of Full Discovery of Evidence

The prosecution and police can coercively gather evidence. This evidence is the property of the citizens, and all of it must be disclosed during a trial. In 1969, the Supreme Court recognized a separate disclosure system, and confined disclosure orders to having a narrow scope. However, in Japan, the prosecution only discloses that which is advantageous to establishing guilt. This contravenes the Constitution and the law, which regard the equality of all parties in principle. Although disclosure has increased following the introduction of trials by lay judges, this is not full disclosure and is insufficient. In 2001, the report of the Judicial Reform Council recommended the introduction of trials by lay judges and legislation for a discovery system. Although the text was drafted in 2004, it did not adopt a 'right of access to evidence of innocence' and an 'obligation for the prosecution to disclose evidence of innocence' as various other countries have. As such, the text remains lacking [25].

4. Adoption of 'Beyond a Reasonable Doubt'

In Japan, it is considered that, as in America, 'beyond a reasonable doubt is a fundamental principle', as seen in a Supreme Court judgment (1975) and the publications of scholars on criminal procedural law that regard a 'presumption of innocence', that 'those suspected will not be punished', and a 'high probability'. However, it is evident that this view has not permeated throughout Japan's penal judges. The principle that 'if the true criminal escapes, a false charge will not be delivered' has not been consistent. The police prioritize the publicization of a criminal's arrest, and following publicization the situation persists such that it is almost impossible for investigators and judges to overturn it. The position of 'presumption of guilt' from bureaucratic judges has become visible, given that the conviction rate used to be 99.9%, but the acquittal rate has increased in lay judge trials.

Part 3 – Reasons Why Inadequacies Cannot Be Rectified

1. Police and Prosecution

The legal system has continued its prioritization of law and order and dependence on criminal punishment.

The use of a few people as scapegoats for social crises and toughened populism to appease the public has been repeated and become the norm.

2. Special Investigations

The special investigations headquarters within the Public Prosecutors Office deals with especially important matters both with and without police.

Through the arrest, custody, and criminal sanctions of politicians and bureaucrats, they attempt to show a healthy legal society, but their coercive investigative methods have been subject to criticism, especially their attempts to settle the social unrest caused by the collapse of the bubble through criminal punishment.

3. Academic Viewpoints

Following the war, many scholars such as Dando, Tamiya, and Hirano introduced various Western systems for guaranteeing human rights; however, their viewpoints are rarely reflected in practice.

4. Reform of Criminal Investigations

Experts have participated in 'Study Group on the State of Prosecution', 'Special Meeting on the Criminal Justice System in the New Age', and others, and considered reforms of prosecution and the criminal justice system. However, these have not reached the resolution of complete transparency and disclosure of evidence for all cases of interrogation.

Part 4 – Trial by Lay Judges

Trials including lay judges (3 judges, 6 lay judges) began from 2009. Examination into improving the system has begun based on the 5-year period of implementation thus far [26].

1. Rise in the Rate of Acquittals

There have been definite results, as evidenced by the rise in acquittals (around 0.5% or 30/6000); the rate of acquittals in judge-only trials was less than 0.01%.

2. The Defendant's Right to Choose

The system should be reformed so that the defendant has a right to select a trial by lay judges, regardless of the seriousness of the crime.

3. Decision Process

Since the obligation on lay judges to keep secrets is too strict (criminal punishment), the discussions for the reform of lay judges system is impossible and the heavy mental burden placed on them is problematic. There is likely a way to gradually lift the ban via soft law in groups whose purpose is to hold this discussions.

Chapter 3

Reform of the Civil Trial

Part 1 – Shortcomings of the Civil Trial

1. The Necessity of Strengthening Relief for Damage

The purpose of the civil trial is to provide quick relief and monetary compensation to people who suffer from unjust acts, breaches of contract, and legal violations. However, the development of civil litigation has lagged and the relief for victims has been insufficient in Japan.

Japan's civil trial system was established around 100 years ago, and was modelled on the German system. It was liberalistic code of legal procedure in which the parties were equal, but the law actually favored stronger parties who had weapons (money, evidence, etc.) over the weak. However, following this, the social civil action and the Stuttgart Model developed in Germany to provide relief to socially and economically weak citizens and workers. There were also significant reforms that 'changed the burden of proof, presumed negligence, and expanded document submission orders' in accordance with an inquisitorial system of justice with the principle of collaboration. Although researchers in

Japan have introduced all these concepts, reforms have not been enacted [e].

In America as well, the civil trial went through explosive development accompanying the expansion of civil discovery. However, Japan does not have the judicial activism of America, nor its adversarial legalism (below) that supports responsive law [27].

(1) Civil Jury

(2) Discovery

(3) Punitive Damage, Treble Damage

(4) Class Action

(5) Preponderance of Evidence (in Japan, the burden of proof on the plaintiff/victim is as high as 70-80%)

In conclusion, compared with the West, the functions of the civil trial in Japan are weak, and there is the tendency to rely on criminal punishment for conflict resolution.

2. The Necessity of Expanding the Discovery of Document

The essence of the trial system is a determination of truth or falsehood on the basis of clear facts. Full discovery of evidence becomes necessary for this purpose. Document submission orders in the old Civil Procedures Act only recognized four kinds of limitations. A small number of scholars and I advocated the introduction of America's discovery system. As the next best option, I presented a reform proposal for promoting the real discovery of evidence by the submission of the written statements of the parties involved and the reports of related parties. The courts substantially adopted this, and major reform was made via soft law. In 1996, the text of the Civil Proceedings Act was amended, and in principle, document submission orders became widely recognized. However, the operation of the courts following this remained largely unchanged. Without cases being clarified, a state of affairs in which unsatisfactory judgments are dealt has continued for the reasons below.

(1) The burden on a judge increases with the volume

of document, so judges limit document to the minimum necessary.

(2) If the parties say that they have lost the document, or that it does not exist or has been destroyed, there is no submission order.

(3) Judges dismiss submissions as 'unnecessary'. In Japan, the system is such that witness questioning, verification, and expert opinion can all be dismissed as 'unnecessary', not just documents. There is no need to issue reasons for the dismissal, and there is no procedure to seek redress for harm suffered by an act of the courts. However, this reason does not hold for documents; this kind of evidence can be examined quite easily. The uniform operating practices of the courts (soft law) have resulted in a constitutional violation.

Part 2 – The Necessity of Expanding Proportionate Liability

1. Expansion in the Tort Law

In Japan traffic accidents occurred so frequently that it was called a 'traffic war'. It was a car society in which people could become both the perpetrator and the victim. Furthermore, in many cases cause and responsibility fell on the victim. Then cases in which responsibility was proportionately divided on the basis of comparative negligence increased in number [c]. Bar Associations took the lead, and constructed a chart depicting many different types of comparative negligence, with the opinions of insurance companies and the courts taken into account. This was an establishment as soft law. However, due to tragic, unabated traffic accidents that resulted in injury or death caused by drunk driving, laws strengthening punishment were established in the form of the crimes of negligent driving and reckless driving causing injury or death.

2. Contract Law and the Principle of Good Faith

Methods for resolving comparative negligence have increased in all areas of unjust acts. That being so, in the area of contract law, the way of thinking of comparative negligence is not adopted. For instance, there have been many cases where, in the case of business dealings of an agent, there is responsibility on the part of both the principal and the trading partner, yet unreasonable judgments of 100 or 0% blame have continued. Reasonable conclusions can be obtained if the 'principle of good faith' in Article 1 of the Civil Code is made use of [28]. However, there is no escape from legal formalism [c].

Part 3 – The Necessity to Strengthen the Functions of Legal Policy

1. From Social Responsibility to Legal Responsibility (America)

According to Nonet and Selznick, in America responsive

law overcame autonomous law and developed as judicial activism under the emergence of social advocacy, which pursues the purposes of public policy.

R.A. Kagan termed America's legal society 'adversarial legalism'[29]. This holds that 'the formation and implementation of policy is not by the bureaucratic administration, but through litigation led by lawyers', and so the judiciary is open to new kinds of litigation and political movement. Relief for victims was a historic development in the history of the American judiciary indicating its elevation from a social responsibility to a legal responsibility. Common law relief was held to be insufficient, and broad relief through equity was recommended. It became a tool for realizing public policy as well.

2. No Interference to the Administration (Japan)

By 1988, this American legal development had already been introduced as the 'modern form of litigation, and public litigation' (to include 'system reform litigation') in Japan as well [30]. However, Japanese courts take the position of not interfering in the executive branch; over 99% of the lawsuits that take the executive as the defendant fail, and so such advances in law creation have not been evidenced. Tokyo District Court Administrative Section Chief Justice Masayuki Fujiyama delivered exceptionally numerous judgments against the executive; however, these decisions were altered in the higher courts.

Chapter 4

Administrative Rules (prevention)

Part 1 – Preventative Functions

The criminal law system punishes criminals after the fact; the civil law system relieves victims after the fact. In order to prevent crime and the outbreak of damage the preventative function of the executive has to be relied on. The main role of the administrative power (central&local government) has conventionally been regarded as the making and implementation of laws for the cultivation of industry, fiscal stimulus, social security, etc. together with political parties. The enforcement of law is carried out by the government through a top-down approach, and embodied mostly in the form of notices and notifications: this is referred to as notification administration.

Conversely, preventative legislation lagged incredibly behind the times in relation to pollution, PL, traffic accidents, work-related accidents, damage to investments, natural disasters, etc. The Ministry of the Environment was established in 2001 to prevent pollution, and the Consumer Affairs Agency in 2009 to protect consumers. Although a number of laws for monetary relief were established after the fact, they did not sufficiently carry out preventative functions.

Recently global risks are occurring in the forms of nuclear power disasters, global warming, unrestrained resource development, environmental destruction, war, terrorism, etc. [31]. These are man-made disasters in the sense that they are caused by mankind, but even including tsunami disasters the 'man-made disaster' aspect is strong for both prevention before the incident and measures following the incident. There is a need to strengthen the preventative system centered on the executive, for which end the following methods should be promoted.

1. Preventative Legislation

In the abstract, the notion that the security of citizens, consumers, workers, etc. should be protected by law is possible. However, a preventative measure cannot be taken without evidence of a specific causal relationship. Accordingly, deterrence measures for prevention such as administrative measures (recommendations, correction orders, and cease-and-desist orders) are combined with a publicization system. Even when the cause of damage cannot be proven with a high probability, it should be made clear that measures can be imposed when the degree of proof is around 50-60%.

2. Soft Law

Soft law (guidelines) should be used to flexibly interpret and apply abstract legal texts. Soft law can be applied flexibly, e.g. by strictly imposing measures when the degree of proof is high (e.g. 90%) and moderately imposing them when it is low (e.g. 55%).

3. Deterrence Measures for Prevention

When the degree of proof is low, then a recommendation or publicization can be released. In situations when the degree is high, an order to rectify an illegal act or an order to suspend business can be issued. According to the legislation, criminal punishment can be added when these orders are contravened. When there is only a recommendation (warning), there are no specific restrictions placed on its subject. However, in most cases there are also social sanctions through publicization. Specific restrictions are set via rectification and suspension orders, and additional sanctions are effected through publicization.

Part 2 – The Large Development of Administrative Soft Law

1. Externalization Phenomenon

In Japan, cabinet orders (cabinet) and ministerial orders (minister) are drawn up after legislation is enacted in the Diet. These are 'statutory orders' and are legally binding. In contrast, notices, notifications, outlines, and announcements are referred to as 'administrative rules'. Administrative rules are considered to be only legally binding on bureaucrats (internal effects), and not legally binding on citizens (external effects). However, in recent times the idea that they are legally binding (i.e., via an externalization phenomenon) has gained sway [5], and the use of the term 'guidelines' has become more widespread. In 1997, in relation to organ transfer, both hard law and soft law were created at the same time with the 'Organ Transplant Law', the 'Organ Transfer

Enforcement Regulations', and their 'Guidelines'.

Administrative rules do not differ from the principles of hard law because legal force is conferred from observing precedent (self-binding), the principle of equality, and from predictability [4]. However, administrative legislation (the soft law from statutory orders and administrative rules) differs from parliamentary law (hard law), and in a modern society it should be variable, tentative, and multiform, according to the situation. The characteristics of soft law should be employed even if doing so reduces the observation of precedent, the principle of equality, and predictability. Furthermore, 'administrative guidance' was civilized in Administrative Procedure Act for the first time in the world in 1993, and was recognized as soft law. Administrative soft law also gains legal force through organizational decisions.

2. Publicization

So that notices and notifications were not publicized, it was often the case that only particular interested parties knew of them, and that the public at large could not investigate them. In 1993, publicization became mandated with the

Administrative Procedure Act. Notifications and guidelines set by government agencies have mostly become accessible through the widespread use of the internet in the 21st century. As a result, it is now possible to take sufficient procedures to examine changes that follow the establishment of guidelines.

Part 3 – The Democratic Operation of Administrative Soft Law

Over a long period of time, bureaucrats operated administrative soft law in a one-sided and closed manner. Furthermore, there were many cases in which soft law was abandoned for no longer suiting the society as the years passed. Unlike hard law, the more soft law is specified, the more contradictions arise, and sections of vacuum become apparent. Procedures that reflect the standpoint of the citizens were made to respond to these issues.

1. Administrative Procedure Act

In 1993, the Administrative Procedure Act was established

to gauge the 'guarantee of fairness' and 'progress towards transparency' in the administrative runnings of the country and of local public entities. This Act obligates government agencies to set examination standards for requests in administrative procedures (e.g., permission and authorization, and administrative guidance). Before disadvantageous measures are taken, there is a 'production of reasons', and a 'hearing process' is guaranteed in order to protect the rights and interests of the measures' subjects.

In addition, in relation to 'administrative guidance' it is now the case that citizens can 'request written service', not just spoken. Because the operation of executive soft law is made more transparent, considerable debate by all kinds of groups can lead to the improvement of soft law [32].

2. Public Comment Procedure (Procedure for Public Opinion)

A characteristic of soft law is that it can be made quickly to respond to changes in society and flexibly reformed. The Public Comment Procedure (procedure for public opinion) was decided by the Cabinet in 1999 in order to improve the top-down administration of notifications. In 2005, it was made law in Chapter 6 of the amended Administrative Procedure Act. The opinions of the general public are sought when soft law is established or modified, not just the opinions of interested parties. The object of the procedure was also broadened to cover 'orders, etc.' (including administrative guidance) that directly relate to the rights and obligations of citizens.

Professor Hisashi Harada conducted an empirical verification of procedures over a 10-year period, and noted that: (1) there were few cases in which the Public Comment Procedure had been implemented; (2) there were few opinions received for any one case of procedure; and (3) there was a low percentage of cases that went to on to be amended after opinions had been received [33]. In response to this, it was considered necessary for a reform proposal that afforded (1) prioritization, (2) increase in activity, and (3) increase in transparency.

3. Petition Confirmation Procedure Prior to Application of the Law

This was introduced with reference to America's no-action letter, which was established by Cabinet decision and is not a law. The Cabinet decision reads, '[i]n relation to specific acts related to their own business activities, which private companies and others are trying to realize, private companies and others confirm whether or not the concerned act is the object of application of specific legal regulations beforehand with a competent administrative body of the concerned regulations. In addition to providing a response, the guidelines for the procedure of publicizing the concerned response are set below'.

In relation to the interpretation of laws and regulations, if the response is thought strange, then a different interpretation can be made by various organizations and discussed with the relevant government agency. In other words, the procedure has made a free discussion of soft law possible.

Part 4 – Civil Control of Administrative Soft Law

The ideal way to reform administrative implementation standards (soft law) to meet new eras is by smoothly changing them through cooperation between the government and the people. However, an active complementary role played by the courts is also considered necessary.

1. Invalidity and Injunction Claims (The Limits of Administrative Discretionary Power)

Prior to the war, the general rule for courts was not to conduct review of the discretionary actions of the executive. However, following the war, Article 30 of the Administrative Litigation Act allowed courts to nullify an administrative measure(decision) when the 'discretionary power had been exceeded or abused': namely, 'when a measure significantly lacked validity from a social perspective'. However, plaintiff lawsuits to have measures found invalid were almost completely rejected.

Judicial review expanded in 1993 because of the

establishment of the Administrative Procedure Act. This expansion came about through the publicization of the creation of standards of review and standards for disciplinary measures by the Agency for Disciplinary Measures. In 2004, the Administrative Litigation Act was revised, establishing litigation endowed with mandates and injuctions.

The social problems that arose because the Japanese national flag and national anthem remained the same after the war are given as an example. Public school teachers were ordered in a notification to 'stand to the national flag and to sing the national anthem with piano accompaniment'. Teachers who refused to do so suffered wage reductions, teaching suspensions, and so on, causing much litigation for revoking the order. While some plaintiffs were successful in district courts, none were successful in the Supreme Court. Among these cases, a landmark case in a district court deserves special mention, where the district court upheld 'the claim that standing, singing, and accompaniment were non-compulsory' (verification of invalidity) and 'the claim for an injunction against the disciplinary measures taken'. This was a civil litigation that took place prior to the plaintiffs receiving disciplinary punishment, and the fact that the court allowed the plaintiff's claims is remarkable when compared to past precedent. The ruling recognized a preventive function in relation to disputes as well as relief on the condition of the invalidity of a notification. This was the birth of preventative relief by the judiciary, which could resolve a dispute before authority suppression of an opposition movements and disciplinary punishment. However, the plaintiff verdict was reversed and their claims unrecognized in the high courts and Supreme Court (2012). In conclusion, it can be said that the legal system is making progress, yet implementation of law stagnates.

However, there has been some progress as a result of a Supreme Court decision in 2012 in relation to the spread of Internet sales of pharmaceutical goods and administrative guidance enforcing face-to-face sales. The plaintiff traders claimed that prohibition of Internet sales exceeded the mandate of the Pharmaceutical Affairs Law, and the Supreme Court recognized their claims of its invalidity in 2013.

2. State Compensation Claims

It is currently extremely rare that the plaintiff is successful in state compensation claims. Under the State Redress Law, so long as an individual bureaucrat follows administrative regulations, then state is under no obligation to pay compensation as a general rule. This is the case even if the administrative regulation is provisionally found illegal or invalid. However, as administrative regulations are relatively flexible, bureaucrats have an obligation not to implement them in a rigid manner, as well as an obligation to avoid causing harm to citizens. When administrative regulations are illegal or invalid or their implementation by a bureaucrat is illegal, then an obligation to pay compensation arises as an illegal act of the state or municipality. However, in such a case it is not the act of the bureaucrat as an individual that is being charged, but rather the state's ongoing liability as an organization. The act should be considered an illegal act by a legal person. So long as there is no malicious intent, the responsibility of a bureaucrat is not questioned at all in Japan.

Chapter 5

Self-Governing Rules

Part 1 – The Role of Private Soft Law

1. The New Role of Intermediary Groups

In 1840, de Tocqueville considered political associations and civil associations, not the individual, as the social units necessary to replace the monarchy and aristocracy. This freedom of association, in addition to the jury system, was seemed to be a foundation of America's democracy [7]. Paul Hirst also advocated associative democracy in 1994 [34].

Civil organizations make and operate soft law outside the state bodies of lawmaking, administration, and justice. Private soft law also must be flexible so that it conforms to social and economic change and legal reform. The bearer of responsibility falls under the umbrella of 'intermediary groups', but they exist in great numbers, as seen below.

Public interest groups (profession groups, specialist groups, labor union federations, conferences, etc.)

Regional groups (residents' associations, town assemblies,

apartment associations, etc.)

Private groups (corporations, labor union, PTAs, etc.)

Formerly intermediary groups functioned to protect their vested interests, and began to make soft law for the purpose of restricting entry into their groups. Today, in order to keep the freedom of business as constitutional right and protect consumers, the reduction of administrative regulations and the strengthening of the Antimonopoly Act have made progress. The National Federation of Agricultural Co-operative Associations, the Federation of Electric Power Companies, and the Japan Medical Association are said to have the most rigid regulations, but there remain many other bodies with barriers to entry. Now obligations have arisen for intermediary groups to exercise soft law for the purposes of citizens as well as consumers and for charitable purpose in line with regulatory reforms. Industry groups have also begun to protect public interests via self-regulation [35].

2. The Social Adaptive Function of Soft Law

Generally, soft law can be called an interpretative rule and implementation rule for the specifics of operating a law. However, in modern day Japan, its most important role is the creation of rules that flexibly conform to social change and economic development [36]. Law has the tendency not to adapt to society as the years pass. Soft law is easily modified and adjustable, and possesses flexibility since the interpretation of law changes bit by bit. Additionally, the soft law of intermediary groups possesses multiformity, as it can differ from group to group. Soft law has a preventative function, which can be called novelty, because it can cope rapidly with new social phenomena. Soft law can also be said to have a reforming function, as it can bit by bit cause a bad law to become a mere scrap of paper.

Article 21 of the Medical Practitioners Act (1906) stipulates that 'police must be notified when a physician has found abnormalities on a dead body', whereupon it becomes a criminal matter. For a long time, notifications were delivered when there was a crime by a third party, but it was established practice not to notify the authorities for cases of medical malpractice. However, patient relief did not make progress in civil trials despite the frequent occurrence of medical malpractice and fabrication of clinical charts. In 1999, a patient died at a high-quality municipal hospital as a result of a mistake where antiseptic solution was put in the intravenous drip solution at the time of surgery. The Supreme Court delivered a decision of guilty, calling the error a violation of the previously dead-letter Article 21. After this ruling, there was an increase in the number of instances of doctors being indicted for medical malpractice. I proposed the formation of soft law that would obligate physicians to notify a third party institution created by medical associations and societies, which would publicize the findings, whereby Article 21 would become a mere scrap of paper once again [b].

In Germany and America, the police do not interfere in places of medicine, much less pursue the criminal punishment of doctors for medical malpractice (with the exception of circumstances where there is intent). This is because medical associations operate strong soft law for patients based on their own strong self governing rule and democratic procedures. In the regulations of the American Medical Association, it is stipulated that 'medical ethics have preference over law'. This is a wonderful regulation. The medical associations of America and Germany are voluntarily striving to improve the state of medicine, including by using the third-party institutions I recommended.

Professor Shōzō Ōta says that the 'separation between law and justice is becoming clear' [38]. Thus, the function of soft law conforming to society is an effort to bring law closer to justice. This is because old law should be brought into line with to the justice of the era, the justice of the region, and the justice of the group.

3. Self-Government and Self-Rule

Soft law must be something that implements justice, virtue, and constitutional values. What are its contents? What are its processes? The thinking below is completely in line with its implementation.

In relation to the justification for governmental authority, Shigenori Matsui contends that modern welfare state-style liberalism should operate by pluralism, in which groups (associations) form, the political participation of citizens is assumed, and the political participation is guaranteed. On this basis, a political community will make determinations at certain times through the alliances of groups with different interests [39]. He holds that as factions and groups seek only private interests, a process must be provided to prevent infringements of the public good and various rights.

Michael Sandel seeks the formation of 'citizen virtues' in communities that include many intermediary groups. Essentially, he comparatively examines liberalism (which seeks to realize the liberal welfare state) and libertarianism (a kind of neoliberalism) with an eye to the principle of majority rule, utilitarianism (which seeks to realize the maximum amount of happiness in the largest amount of people), and the principle of protecting the rights of minorities. In libertarianism, he argues, citizens are completely disconnected in a world in which the individual is totally independent; in liberalism, the individual relies too much on the state and loses independence. As such, Professor Sandel advocates a pluralistic and decentralized-authority republicanism centering on many kinds of communities, while continuing to respect the principles of majority rule, utilitarianism, and protecting rights [40]. Accordingly, he holds that the establishment of 'self-government' and 'self-rule' also become possible. As a result, 'citizenship and cooperation' can be secured and each person's interests, rights, and equality shall be regulated and justice will take shape through careful deliberation, by no means through only one majority decision in the community.

In this book, I have assumed that the public good is the target of administrative soft law and the soft law of public interest groups. Furthermore, notwithstanding the interests of companies and various groups, the mass media, social networks, and the like lack value so long as the interests of the citizens, consumers, and workers are ignored. There are cases where excessively pursuing private interests leads to violations of hard and soft law, and to outflows of social criticism, compensation claims, and criminal punishment. I wish to emphasize that soft law should be treated as a constitutional norm in Japan, and deliberated on carefully and operated flexibly.

Part 2 – The Justifiability of Civil Soft Law (Legal Binding Force)

1. The Legitimacy of Civil Soft Law

(1) Substantial justifiability

Soft law cannot violate the constitutional values; in other words, it cannot encroach upon fundamental human rights and social rights. In principle, soft law that violates various rights is invalid. Soft law must be changed intra-organizationally since much of it in Japan is old, irrational, and invalid.

(2) Procedural justifiability

In intermediary groups, soft law that has been passed via a just procedure has procedural justifiability. In other words, justifiability rises the more accurate information is released, the longer soft law is deliberated on, and the more a majority vote is repeated.

2. Binding Force – Strengths and Weaknesses

The binding force of public soft law is generally strong. When a taxation notification is contravened, there are many related criminal punishments. The binding force of private soft law is generally weak compared with public soft law. However, it is misleading to explain that private soft law lacks binding force generally. For instance, treatment guidelines have vigor because they are used as the basis for civil compensation claims as a reason to target hospitals for medical malpractice [41].

3. (Effective) Methods of Sanction

When civil soft law has both procedural justifiability and substantial justifiability, the following sanctions are effective, and the soft law functions satisfactorily as a reference.

(1) Soft law in the form of safety regulations to protect consumers who create a public interest group and patients serves as reference for compensation claims.

(2) (1) above serves as reference for injunctions.

(3) In an organization, soft law serves as reference for the suspension of qualifications or expulsion from a group of a member who breaks a regulation.

(4) A standard public announcement concerning the offender (highly effective via the internet).

4. Judicial Review (Ineffective Cases)

The following legal claims can be reasons for a soft law's invalidity.

(1) Claim requesting an injunction or invalidity confirmation of soft law itself targeting a group itself.

(2) Compensation claim against a group or its members

(3) Claim of invalid suspension of qualifications or expulsion (abuse of discretionary power)

It is very rare for a court to find private soft law invalid by way of (1), (2), or (3) above, even if it contravenes constitutional freedoms and rights. So long as a group's majority vote procedures are in order, then there will not be an examination into its substantive justification because of the theory of 'self control community', which respects the self-rule of groups. Almost the only exception to this was a Supreme Court decision to rule invalid a decision to expel a Jehovah's Witness high school student who would not participate in kendo practice because of their doctrine of total pacifism. The finding of invalidity was decided because the principal's decision was found to be remarkably lacking in social sensibilities of appropriateness, as well as an abuse of the principle's discretionary power [D].

The most important example that demonstrates Japan's backwardness is that of a case in 2004 when Doctor Ōtani was disbarred from the Japan Society of Obstetrics and Gynecology for carrying out a preimplantation genetic diagnosis [g]. The courts allowed neither the doctor's claim for invalidity of the expulsion and reinstatement of status, nor the patient's claim for compensation [E]. PGD began in England and America from 1990 and spread throughout the world [h]. In Germany, the Medical Association released an announcement of opposition (soft law) in relation to its legal prohibition (criminal punishment), and in 2010 doctors who carried out PGD were found to be innocent [F]. Although the Japan Society of Obstetrics and Gynecology was successful in court, it lost in the case's media coverage and public opinion, and Doctor Ōtani was allowed to rejoin the Society. In 2006, the Society accepted PGD as to structure abnormality. Investigations into the pros and cons of preimplantation genetic diagnosis screening began this year [k][d].

Part 3 – Safety Regulations and Consumer Protection

1. Regulation Reforms

(1) Entry Regulations

Entry regulations through administrative permission and authorization, and admission refusal by business groups took place in every industrial field over a long period in Japan. For a long period, the Antimonopoly Act did not function. Entry regulations are now becoming smoother through the enactment of regulative reforms and retraction orders by the Fair Trade Commission of Japan.

(2) Cartels

A leniency system for cartels was legislated in 2006, which has eventually started to become effective. To some degree, cases in which the Japan Fair Trade Commission imposes surcharges have increased; however, such cases remain few.

(3) Safety Regulations

Consultations and agreements between groups become important. Entry regulations and cartel regulations are not permitted. However, situations where groups cannot change because of established practices over a long period also occur. It should be made unambiguous that the role of each group is to strive for safety regulations for consumer protection.

(4) Judicial Review

For the most part, courts have not recognized claims for injunctions and damage compensation in relation to violations of the Antimonopoly Act and administrative soft law that interfered in business. In 2011, a district court recognized a compensation claim for a convenience store's headquarters constraining the trade of its resellers, in direct contravention to Article 19 of the Antimonopoly Act. Also in 2011, a district court upheld an injunction claim in relation to unjust interference with dry-ice trade citing Article 24 of the Antimonopoly Act.

2. Consumer Trial Procedures Special Law

(1) Direct Claims by Consumers

There are not many cases of direct claims by individual consumers in Japan and the damages recovered are small, because there are no class-action or three-times damage systems.

(2) Claims by Groups

The Consumer Justice Procedure Special Law (established in 2013, operational within three years) allows a specially qualified consumer group to make a claim on behalf of multiple victims. However, a large exception was carved out with the exclusion of physical suffering, extended damages, lost profit compensation, consolation money, etc.

Chapter 6

Fiscal Spending in the Social State

Part 1 – Fiscal Spending

1. Fiscal Expenditure

Beginning with state-owned companies in the Meiji period, socialism, the influence of militarism, and the post-war priority production system have continued to cause fiscal spending to be extremely high. Social security expenses increased under a welfare state. The expansion continued because of the spending policies of Keynesian economics and fiscal spending to stimulate growth.

The outline of the government budget for the 2014 period is as follows.

(1) Annual revenue: 96,000,000,000,000 yen

Tax revenue: 50,000,000,000,000 yen; issuance of government bonds: 41,000,000,000,000 yen; other: 5,000,000,000,000 yen

(2) Annual expenditure: 96,000,000,000,000 yen

Public project expenses: 6,000,000,000,000 yen; social security expenses: 31,000,000,000,000 yen; education expenses: 5,000,000,000,000 yen; national defense expenses: 5,000,000,000,000 yen; repayment of government bonds: 23,000,000,000,000 yen

(3) Primary balance: (basic financial income)

(96 – 23) – (96 – 41) = 18   18,000,000,000,000 yen deficit

(4) Public and other debts: around 1,000,000,000,000,000 yen

(5) Consumption taxes 1989, 3% → 1997, 5% → 2014, 8% → 2015 predicted at 10% (subject to improvements in the state of the economy)

(6) Legal binding force: Taxes are collected extremely strictly and the imposition of pension payments continues to be strengthened. On the other hand, in relation to annual expenditures, the actual situation is unclear because

fraudulent receipt is almost completely unchecked and because enforcement cannot be strengthened.

2. Public Project Expenses

Public project expenses fell in 2009 under the DPJ, and increased in 2012 under the LDP. For those who receive public project expenses, equality and fairness in the bidding process have been harmed by the bid-rigging of parties with vested interests. This is a violation of the Antimonopoly Act. Bid-rigging exposed by the Fair Trade Commission of Japan is only a portion of the total. Furthermore, construction costs pass from the original contractor to primary subcontractors, to secondary subcontractors, to tertiary subcontractors, and then to the workers. Less and less is allocated to individual subcontractors and workers. Fraudulent behavior has been prevalent in relation to radioactive decontamination operations, wherein businessmen under contract by the state or regional autonomous bodies take money without actually performing decontamination.

3. Social Security Expenses

Social security expenses have continued to expand, and have reached 40% including education expenses. These cover an incredibly broad range of domains, including welfare benefits, medicine, nursing care, childcare, unemployment measures, etc. The unjust receipt of assistance money is widespread. Welfare benefits are being acquired by false claims of physical injury and depression. In 2013, the Welfare Benefit Law was amended, taking a policy of preventing dishonest behavior. On the other hand, trials aimed at improving welfare benefits began in 1957; 15 plaintiff lawsuits were even filed this year.. Article 25 of the Constitution guarantees 'minimum standards of a healthy and cultured lifestyle'.

Academic theories regarding this include the theory of provisional rights, the theory of specific rights, and the theory of abstract rights. The Diet has established laws for livelihood protection, and the Supreme Court has rejected all claims because the executive provides specific standards that are interpreted as within its discretionary scope. If regulations are operated with the injection of soft law characteristics—by establishing specific standards based on careful investigation, by differentiating among regions and age-groups, by having many people participate, etc.— the consent of the people can be obtained.

Part 2 – Countermeasures for Improper Receipt

1. The improper receipt of financial expenditures is widespread, and its methods are hidden and ingenious. It is incredibly difficult for the bureaucrats granting benefits to expose this. This is because bureaucrats cannot spend the time and effort to undertake the relevant investigations; and, because blame can fall on the bureaucrats themselves even if improper conduct is discovered for officials who were insufficiently supervised during their investigation. If even a portion is returned, then criminal charges are not pursued, nor is the behavior made public. This cannot result in general prevention, and malicious individuals continue to offend. Unjust deception continues to spread, and those who do not receive welfare benefits improperly tend to suffer a loss. This should be prevented by means of anonymous reporting

systems and incentives. The method of whistle-blowing is effective for dealing with the improper acts and tax evasion of companies. Investigations hold enormous costs for the police and governmental agencies. Thus, investigations can take place more effectively if benefits are granted to whistle-blowers. Not only that, but cases are anticipated to be preventable before they become big through early detection.

2. America's Conscientious Employee Protection Act allows claims for: (1) injunctions for retaliatory measures; (2) reinstatement of an employee's status; (3) compensation for e.g. loss of wages (including compensation for disciplinary measures); and (4) fines for employers [42]. On the other hand, in Japan there were opinions that a whistle-blowing system would be bad. Nonetheless, the Whistleblower Protection Law was established in 2004 and has been in force since 2006. Yet despite the introduction of the American system, the law remains restrictive as it seeks to avoid damage taken by companies themselves. In America a worker who has made an accusation is protected not only in cases where there is an illegal act, but in cases where "it is rationally believed that there is a high probability of an illegal act occurring".

In Japan, the legal text has not been drafted to this extent; however, the law must operate so that it can be broadly interpreted and it is easy for whistle-blowers to report claims.

America has also passed the False Claims Act, which allows anyone to seek compensation from a company or person that has caused the federal government damage as a result of a false claim, with a possible amount of 15-30% of the total compensation to the government.

Part 3 – Systems for the Disclosure of Information

From the 1980s in Japan, campaigns driven by lawyers, journalists, and scholars took place over a long period. Lagging behind the West, the Access to Government Information Act was established in 1999. Information disclosure offices were set up in the government and local self-governing bodies, and a degree of disclosure was accomplished. However, the disclosure exceptions for defense, foreign affairs, etc. are extremely rigid.

Furthermore, the Protection of Personal Information Law was established in 2003. The situation was that banks were not disclosing the information of debtors and patients. As the acquisition of this information is a right of debtors and patients, the law made it clear that such information should be disclosed. However, it is a rule in society that in principle an individual's information should not be disclosed. This is a limitation on broader operation of the Access to Government Information Act.

Furthermore, this was greatly limited by the establishment of the Special Secrecy Law in 2013. Currently, the Japan Bar Association is suggesting that disclosure should be on the basis of the Global Principles on National Security and the Right to Information.

The Information Disclosure Law has no provisions for in-camera trials. The Fukuoka High Court had effectively recognized in-camera trials through a confirmation ruling, but the Supreme Court did not allow it. An amended law to introduce in-camera trials was scrapped in 2012 [43].

Part 4 – The Medical Insurance System

Medical insurance operates by administrative soft law via notices and bulletins. The system has many problems; two recent examples will be given.

1. Concerning the Reduction in Compensation for Residents of the Same Building

The practice of elderly care facilities requesting and collecting patient referral fees from visiting doctors is widespread. As this system damages the purposes of medical insurance, the Ministry of Health, Labour and Welfare took sudden measures to stop it. Specifically, in April 2016 the integrated administrative fee for house calls (remuneration calculated once a month, for two or more continuous visits per month) for patients who reside in the same building will be revised and reduced to 1/4 of an equivalent house call at a single residence, and the patient referral fee will be revised and reduced from the current 1/4 (for single residences) to around 1/8.

The characteristics of continuity, certainty, clarity, equality, and predictability are present in all standards. However, this practice not only greatly harms these characteristics, but significantly destroys predictability for no reason.

Accordingly, this kind of predictability-damaging theory of course does not exist in fields outside medicine, or in actual practice. For instance, there has long been the principle of prohibiting detrimental changes regarding wages realized both in theory and in practice: even under conditions of deflation, more than gradual reductions of 3% or 5% have been permitted, and even this is exceptional. For rent reduction as well, a method of staged reduction with 5% or 10% set as the limit is taken in the actual practice of arbitration courts. In addition, concerns are limited to inflation indexing for cases of livelihood protection costs and pension decisions.

In other words, despite the opposition of medical personnel, the government has largely led policy on house calls by new establishments and additions to the medical service payment system. As a result, a system is being created in which treatment can be received sufficiently and impartially whether at home or in group facilities. However, from the doctors' point of view, one can point out that that the effort expended for a medical examination in group housing cannot possibly be considered 1/4 of that of a medical examination at a home. If this large reform is allowed then examinations in group facilities will be severely constrained. In such a situation, mobility-impaired patients who need emergency treatment will have no choice but to abandon hope for treatment simply because they live in a group facility.

This is clearly no more than discriminatory treatment between patients who live at home and patients in group facilities, and shows a complete lack of fairness. It also lacks consistency, turning upside-down the government's earlier policy of introducing comprehensive regional care. Furthermore, the faith of citizens in medical treatment will be threatened because of the great damage to the predictability of their medical treatment.

2. Concerning the 16-km Limit for House Calls

Conventionally, claims for remuneration for medical

treatment from health insurance are not recognized in principle in relation to house calls when the distance between the authorized insurance medical institution and the patient exceeds 16 kilometers, and the region is not clearly an area lacking doctors with a Number 1 or Number 2 region designation by the Minister of Health, Labor and Welfare. However, this 16-km limit is aimed at policing coming and going into other districts in the name of safety regulations. It is a completely illogical, extremely old rule, which no longer conforms to the status quo. Moreover, in modern Japan with its developed transportation, there are no longer any regions that satisfy the requirements to be designated a Number 1 or Number 2 regions.

Accordingly, there is a need for new soft law that replaces the 16-km limit: specifically, law that recognizes multiformity in terms of regions. Cities and mountain villages should be considered separately. While on the one hand predictability is important, the operation of soft law must also be flexible so that it can be a benefit to people's lifestyles and lead to legal reform. Since the 16-km limit clearly causes no disadvantages to anyone but patients in the countryside and on islands, exceptions must be established and the law leniently operated. In other words, the 16-km limit ought to be exceed-able when the need is high for patients in the countryside. Even lacking this need, if the 16-km limit is exceeded, it should suffice if compensation is given less the fraction by which it was exceeded. However, like other cases of compensation repayments, the fear surfaces of measures forcing the return of all compensation for such patients who received examination or treatment. If this measure is allowed, then doctors who are earnestly and selflessly devoted to their patients cannot obtain insurance earnings through providing at-home treatment to patients who live far away. It is clear that such a situation cannot sustain medicine aimed at patient relief, and thus that this measure is unlawful and unreasonable.

Since the 16-km rule is an illogical limit it has been operated loosely for a long time. However, there is now a movement to strengthen this regulation, along with the shared-facility regulation discussed above, because of developments in transportation in urban areas making it faster to get to shared facilities. However, the situation for medical treatment is completely different in the countryside and on islands. There is a need for soft law to operate in a way that matches its actual place and region.

Chapter 7

The Right to Vote and Political Parties

Part 1 – From Two Large Political Parties to Multiple Parties

In modern constitutional law, which includes the Japanese Constitution, the freedom of association is guaranteed and the role of political parties is viewed with importance. A political party's manifesto (i.e., stipulation of goals), administrative rules, resolution items, and so forth have legal effect as soft law. When a member is expelled, if there has been no substantial violation of soft law as set by the political party, then a court will regard the expulsion as an abuse of discretionary power and thus invalid, and continue to recognize the qualifications of the member. In recent times, warnings, revocation of qualifications, and expulsions have been used against party members. The courts consider these actions valid as they fall within the party's scope of discretionary power, so long as there is no substantial violation of soft law set by the political party. Thus, party members do not dispute such measures through litigation. For this reason, some criticize that, compared to America, the binding nature of party decisions in Japan is excessively strong.

In Japan party politics developed from before the war, and grants are made in proportion to the number of parliamentarians as a result of the 1995 Law for Government Subsidies of Political Parties. The proportional representation system that had multiple candidates in medium-sized constituencies was changed in 1994 to mainly a one-person election system in single-seat constituencies in order to encourage two-party politics. Roughly, the conservative party (the present-day LDP) that has maintained power over a long period has been in opposition once. Furthermore, although the Democratic Party of Japan won a majority in the House of Representatives in 2009, the Liberal Democratic Party continued to have a majority in the House of Councilors, leading to a situation of divided government. In 2012, there was a dissolution of parliament and a general election was held in which the Liberal Democratic Party came to majority in both Houses. The DPJ fell into the minority, and other many minority parties flooded the political scene.

It became clear that party politics by two main parties had failed in Japan, and that Japan should aim for a multiple party system (3~4 parties) and ruling coalitions, as in England

and Germany. The reason for this is that public opinions are diverse, and that much soft law should be examined and improved from various angles. Parties need to connect them independently to various organizations, administrations, regional assemblies, and the parliament in relation to many topics. A proportional representation, multi-party system in medium- and large-sized constituencies is appropriate for this purpose.

Part 2 – Low Voter Turnout and Wasted Votes

Voter turnout in national elections is low despite Japan being a major economic and educational power. Until 10 years ago, voter turnout was around 70%, afterwards falling to around 60%. Voter turnout for regional assemblies is mostly below 50%. Reasons for this include active refusals to vote and apathy. This is especially the case for single-seat electoral systems because voting for a minority party essentially results in a wasted vote, and there has been a consequent increase in people who think that voting is meaningless. In order to reflect the will of the people and begin to create multiform soft law, there is a need to eliminate wasted votes and bring in proportional representation.

Part 3 – Malapportionment (Constitutional Violation)

In Japan, an unprecedented court challenge filed by lawyers submitted that the large difference between the value of a single vote in the House of Representatives and the Senate was unconstitutional. Many lawyers participated, with many determinations that the malapportionment was unconstitutional or that it existed in a 'status of unconstitutionality'. In 2013, the Supreme Court deemed it the latter. There have only been a few cases in which a law has been found to be unconstitutional in Japan. Human rights violations and discrimination had continued over a long time in Japan, but courts did not provide relief to victims, giving the reason that rights can be limited by public welfare. However, there were many district- and high-court judgments finding the difference unconstitutional because malapportionment was an issue that was extremely easy to understand.

However, the Supreme Court took the conservative view of

a 'status of unconstitutionality'. On the other hand, this is no more than a technical issue, which can easily be resolved by dividing electoral districts, or by increasing the quorum. The issue is important as a symbol of the Japanese people being unable to undertake reforms.

Part 4 – Civil Service System Reform

In the government, there is a head office in Tokyo and branch offices in each prefecture. Civil servants do not change, even if the ruling party and ministers do. Likewise, there are civil servants in prefectures, cities, and towns, who work until the retirement age because they enjoy guaranteed employment. The civil service implemented many of the administrative rules that were established after the war in Japan. In relation to the opinions of the advisory council on the topics of deregulation and regulatory reform, the civil service continued opposition by allying with vested interest groups and continued opposition. Prime Minister Junichirō Koizumi embarked on politically driven regulation reform and civil service reform, and the DPJ also tried to advance this agenda, but they met strong resistance by civil servants.

While the current LDP Government have said that they are initiating economic growth (i.e., regulation reforms) through a continuation of monetary easing and implementing fiscal stimulus, these goals cannot materialize. The situation is such that regulation reforms cannot be enacted so long as the public service system is not reformed. Below are two measures for reform.

(1) Personnel exchange with the private sector – transfer 20-30% of all bureaucrats to the private sector for 5-10 years, and conversely send in individuals from the private sector. The lifestyle of private citizens and the trends in the market in government can be reflected in governance, and administrative reform will become possible.

(2) Reform of soft law

Modification of administrative soft law is effected by a bottom-up approach from the private sector, or through policy proposals by political parties. In the private sector as well, the formation of soft law is ideal within processes where consultation with the administration is possible and which provide policies for fair and proper administration. It is through this kind of soft law that legislating for regulation reform can be realized.

Chapter 8

Radiation Damage from the 3.11 Great Earthquake Disaster

Part 1 – Residential Areas that are Difficult to Return to

Recovery from the 1995 Great Hanshin–Awaji Earthquake was accomplished in around 10 years through consensus formation among the local people (i.e., soft law) and new laws [44]*. Recovery from the tsunami damage caused by the 3.11 Great Earthquake disaster is likewise gradually progressing, drawing from the lessons of the Great Hanshin–Awaji Earthquake. However, restoration of the areas that suffered radiation damage as a result of the Fukushima Daiichi nuclear power plant disaster is, with the exception of Hiroshima and Nagasaki, a historic-first experience that is extremely troublesome. Although decontamination operations are taking place at government expense, there has not been any progress. Until now, the policy had been to let all of those who wish to return home to do so. However, the situation at present has induced a division between those who hope to return home and those who will not return and move to a different region. Generally speaking, it is necessary to create soft law concerning the popular will within those three groups. Assistance policies and compensation are supposed to be decided from those considerations, but are not making progress.

Part 2 – Acceptable Levels of Radiation on the Human Body

The annual permissible physical radiation exposure is 1 millisievert (mSv). In the beginning of the incident, the government set the level at 5 mSv; recently it has been trying to set it at 20 mSv. People should examine this issue themselves in their schools, communities, and groups, and each organization should implement their own soft law. More appropriate standards should be set by trialing and modifying various methods. Law will be made when the time comes to confer legal force. These operations would be smooth since this is legislation that can be made through a bottom-up procedure and at the same time there are rules for implementation.

Part 3 – Policy of Abolishing Nuclear Power

1.The opinion that nuclear power should be abolished is spreading among citizens. In particular, the report of the National Diet of Japan Fukushima Nuclear Accident Independent Investigation Commission—chaired by Professor Kiyoshi Kurokawa and which considered the incident a 'man-made disaster'—has been greatly influential both at home and abroad [45]. Following 3.11, all 17 reactors were suspended, including those that undergo regular inspection. As of January 2014, only the Ōi Nuclear Power Plant is operating. Protests take place every Friday by the Diet and by the Prime Minister's official residence. About five political parties recommended the abolishment of nuclear power; the DPJ administration proposed abolishment after 30 years. However, in 2013 the LDP administration decided to restart the nuclear power plants. Many groups and communities in Japan are advocating a suspension of nuclear power plants, and have decided to be uncooperative in regard to their restarting. If they created soft law, it would be to push for the abolition of nuclear power. However, this formation of this kind of soft law has not yet taken place, as people are not aware of such methodologies. At present, former Prime Minister Junichirō Koizumi is advocating the suspension of nuclear power plants because of the difficulties surrounding the disposal of nuclear waste, and is becoming a major influence [46].

2.Until 3.11, resident plaintiffs have won two lower-court lawsuits—one in relation to injunctions for nuclear power stations to cease operation, and one in relation to invalidating the decision to issue a construction permit—but even these lost in a higher-court trial. They have lost 33 other similar lawsuits.

The new lawsuits following 3.11 are attracting special attention. Residents initiated a derivative lawsuit filed as Tokyo Electric Power Company (TEPCO) shareholders and, moreover, criminal proceedings against TEPCO officials for bodily injury through professional negligence. However no indictment was served, and they are now pleading for the case to be heard by the Prosecution Review Commission.

Chapter 9

The Creation of Law and the Innovators of Law

Part 1 – The Inferior Position of the Judiciary

1. The Age of the 20% Judiciary

With the end of the Tokugawa period, the legal and cultural influences of the Netherlands, England, France, Germany, and America entered Japan in the Meiji period (in that order). The trial system was not one by jury, or a joint judge-jury system, but a strong and authoritative prosecutorial system, under which lawyers received separate education and training and acted under the supervision of a judicial officer. There were many violations of human rights, and many anti-war protestors were murdered. However, following the war, a modern constitution containing provisions guaranteeing human rights was established under the guidance of GHQ. Judges, prosecutors, and lawyers received uniform legal education and training and undertook the same bar examination. In form, a fair and equal qualification system was established. With the transition of the disciplinary function (supervisory rights) from the Ministry of Justice to the Bar Association, lawyers gained autonomy, and acquired significant personal security. Although many (4-year) law faculties were established across the country, few people passed the bar examination: around 500 people.

With the structure of collusion between the political world, business world, and bureaucracy, as well as the formation of the convoy method for state administration (regulative administration), the role of the courts was limited to resolving the disputes of individuals and small- to medium-sized companies. Lawsuits against the executive and large companies could not be won, and rarely took place. Furthermore, as associate judicial officers, and related legal experts and specialists (referred to as 'related professionals') were recognized in addition to lawyers, these related professionals took up work outside of courts. Lawyers became restricted to trial work. This narrow scope is known as the 20% judiciary.

2. The Campaign to Reform the Japan Federation of Bar Associations

Many cases of workplace disasters, pollution, PL, and drug-induced suffering took place during the period of rapid high economic growth. Neither Communist Party and Socialist Party nor the trade union federations that supported them were able to achieve relief for victims. As one would expect from a '20% judiciary', its capacity to resolve these issues was small as a consequence of judicial passivism as well as the small number of legal professionals. The Japan Federation of Bar Associations has conducted operations for a long period to promote the substantial rule of law, including a system in which judges are selected from experienced lawyers and other legal experts, and the introduction of a jury system for civil and criminal matters. However, they have not been realized because of opposition by the Ministry of Justice.

Part 2 – Reform of the Judiciary

1. The Recommendations of the Advisory Council for Judicial Reform

From 1990, there were calls by the mass media and the business community for an increase in legal professionals. Neither the Japan Federation of Bar Associations nor the Ministry of Justice agreed. The Advisory Council for Judicial Reform began in 1999. In the Dai-Ni Tokyo Bar Association, focusing on the Committee for Education of Legal Professionals that I chaired, undertook an examination of American law schools, and announced a structure for law schools, which involved selection of judges from experienced lawyers, abolition of the Judicial Research and Training Institute, and a system for training lawyers. In 2001, the Advisory Council for Judicial Reform released a set of recommendations centered on the establishment of law schools and a lay judge system for serious criminal matters. Whether its general remarks, which sang the praises of the 'rule of law', have been substantiated in the 10 years since the appearance of law schools has become an issue [47].

2. The Crisis of Permanentized Related Professionals

There was an increase in both lawyers and related professionals as a result of judicial reforms that took place 10 years ago. While there are around 35,000 lawyers at present, there are around 185,000 related professionals, as seen below. The side assisting regulative administration is strong, and is subject to supervision.

Tax Attorney: 74,000people-tax report (The National Tax Administration Agency)

Judicial Scrivener: 20,000 people – registration applications (Ministry of Justice)

Patent Attorney: 10,000 people – trademark licenses and applications (Agency for Cultural Affairs)

Licensed Social Insurance Consultant: 37,000 people – workforce management and social insurance applications (Ministry of Health, Labor and Welfare)

Administrative Scrivener: 44,000 people – administrative licenses and permits, notification requests (prefectural governors)

The Advisory Council for Judicial Reform allowed a provisional rise in the number of related professionals together with the rise in the number of lawyers, which has led to the serious crisis of these related professionals being made permanent. And yet, most law schools and legal professionals have not begun to debate this at all.

Part 3 – Law School Reform

Ten years have passed since the commencement of law schools, and we are now in a period when reform should take place.

1. The Image of the Legal Profession

The present discussion of what the image of the legal profession is for the purposes of education is being debated. The roles of legal professionals are to 'create law (hard law, soft law)', to 'make law conform to society', and to 'bring law closer to justice'; a legal professional is a reformer and innovator of the law. Soft law was not considered, almost so far as to say completely disregarded, as a subject in previous debates. However, legal professionals must have a unified grasp of hard law, soft law, and other standards, and make efforts to bring law closer to justice. In other words, the distinction is not definite, it is relative [48]. An individual who becomes a legal professional should study the theory behind the creation, modification, and annulment of law, not merely laws at an individual level.

2. Abolition of Related Professionals

Related professionals obtain their qualifications by passing an exam based on a narrow scope of legal knowledge; they are not legal professionals in a general or international sense. Accordingly, related professionals do not play a role in protecting, scrutinizing, or reforming the law. There is a need for legal professionals to enter every area of civil society for the expansion of the rule of law, in particular for reform to responsive law. Historically, related professionals have assumed responsibility for regulative administration, particularly under the supervision of a regulatory agency [49]. It can be said that now, in an age in which regulative reform has become a goal of society, this role has come to an end; that the number of related professionals should decline in line with social change, and the granting of new qualifications should be suspended. Of course, the qualifications of current related professionals will continue. The Japan Association of Law Schools teaches all of the duties of related professionals at law schools, and shoulders the heavy burden of designing their integration into a lawyer's responsibilities. The faculties of law that has educated related professionals hitherto, the faculties of law, should be abolished, and law schools should be qualitatively and quantitatively enriched.

3. Selection of Judges from Trained Lawyers

Following graduation of law school and passing of the Bar Examination, lawyers study current practices; however, these current practices are accepted uncritically in order to pass the graduation exam (the second examination). This cannot cultivate a critical mind. The Supreme Court and the Public Prosecutors Office employ legal trainee who are devoted to the current system. It has been suggested that the Judicial Research and Training Institute be abolished, and that there be a trainee lawyer system with the obligation of a 2-year training period at a legal office as a condition of opening an independent legal practice. Realization of these suggestions is simple, given the example systems of England and Canada to draw from. As trainee lawyer will continue to work following training in a legal office, they will become judges and prosecutors in 5-10 years. A system in which judges are selected from experienced lawyers will be automatically realized. Although this system has been recommended for a long time, its realization will become possible for the first time with an increase in legal professionals and the trainee lawyer system.

4. The Important Role of the Japan Association of Law Schools

Reform of the courts and of judgments could not be accomplished through judicial reform. However, through the expansion of law school education, the Japan Association of Law Schools has the power to effect the abolishment of related professionals, trigger the abolishment of the Judicial Research and Training Institute, and instate judges of the Supreme Court in the manner written below. It is my hope that the Japan Association of Law Schools will lead law schools with the creation of soft law.

Part 4 – Passivism of the Supreme Court

1. Non-use of the Power of Judicial Review

In America, as in Japan, there is the power of judicial review, and Germany and South Korea have constitutional courts. In the above countries, there have been hundreds of decisions finding unconstitutionality; in Japan, there have been no more than around 20 verdicts either finding a law unconstitutional or finding the application of a law unconstitutional. Their content is not worth raising, nor is it of significance to society. For example, one Supreme Court judgment in 2013, which found Article 900 of the Civil Code unconstitutional, was important as conservative process. Article 900 provided that the inheritance of a child born to unmarried parents would be half of that of a child born to married parents. Despite many judgments of lower courts finding unconstitutionality at much earlier stages, the right of such children was denied over a long period, and it was not until after rectification in many other countries that it was finally recognized.

Article 9 of the Constitution provides for the 'renunciation of war' and the 'disavowal of armaments and the right of belligerency'. In 1973, a district court found that the Self-Defense Forces Law violated the Constitution; however, a high court and the Supreme Court found that it did not. In other words, all courts, including district courts, have the power of judicial review. While this power is referred to as 'judicial supremacy', it is clear that to present the emphasis has been on the 'supremacy of the legislature and the executive'. The Constitution, which guarantees fundamental human rights, has not been turned into ideology in form only. Hereafter, I anticipate that the Supreme Court will take a step away from judicial passivism, even if it is only one step.

2. Appointment of Supreme Court Judges

Article 79 of the Japanese Constitution provides that 'judges of the Supreme Court are to be appointed by the Cabinet'. However, in practice, the Supreme Court decides the 15 positions on the basis of background. Two-thirds of the 15 positions are occupied by conservative judges (6 people), prosecutors, (2 people), and bureaucrats (2 people); the remaining one-third is occupied by lawyers (4 people), and a scholar (1 person). Conservatives always have a majority, which is the major factor behind the Court's reliance on judicial passivism, stopping at merely the formal rule of law, and its lack of progress in judicial activism and responsive law.

David S. Law published 'The Japanese Supreme Court and Judicial Review', in which he critically presents the 'Japan's administration of justice from the point of view of American researchers'. In his conclusion, David S. Law proposes that in order to sever the control of the judicial bureaucratic system, 'one constitutional scholar or public law scholar should be appointed to each of the three Petty Benches of the Supreme Court', and that 'an organization of legal scholars or a law school consortium should be allowed to draw up a candidate list' [50]. David S. Law's analysis and proposals suggest to many Japanese people hoping for legal reform, including Japanese legal scholars, that positive reforms through soft power are possible, and the possibilities to walking the road to responsive law.

〈主要な参考文献〉 Main References

1 宮澤節生編集代表「国際犯罪学会第16回世界大会報告集 」, Setsuo Miyazawa eds."The Book of Abstracts"16th World Congress of the International Society for Criminoligy,2011

2 Philippe Nonet and Philip Selznick "Law and Society in Transition:Toward Pesponsive Law"1978, ノネ・セルズニック, 六本佳平訳『法と社会の変動理論』1981,岩波書店

3 BRIAN Z.TAMANAHA"ON THE RULE OF LAW:History,Politics,Theory"2004,CAMBRIDGE UNIVERSITY PRESS, ブライアン・Z・タマナハ, 四本健二監訳『「法の支配」をめぐって－歴史・政治・理論』2011,現代人文社

4 大橋洋一『行政規則の法理と実態』2002,有斐閣, /Yōichi Oohashi, *The Legal Theory and Reality of Administrative Regulation*, 中川丈久『行政手続と行政指導』2000,有斐閣, /Takehisa Nakagawa, *Administrative Procedure and Administrative Guidance : Comparative Law Analysis*

5 宇賀克也『行政法概説Ⅰ－行政法総論【第2版】』2006,有斐閣

6 中山信弘編集代表『ソフトロー研究叢書』2008,有斐閣, 藤田友敬編, 第1巻『ソフトローの基礎理論』、神田秀樹編, 同第2巻『市場取引とソフトロー』、中里実編, 同第3巻『政府規制とソフトロー』、大渕哲也編, 同第4巻『知的財産とソフトロー』、小寺彰編, 同第5巻『国際社会とソフトロー』、東京大学大学院法学政治学研究科２１世紀ＣＯＥプログラム

『ソフトロー研究』第1号～第22号　2005～2013, [Nobuhiro Nakayama eds.,*Soft Law Research Library* , Tomotaka.Fujita eds *Volume 1: The Foundational Theory of Soft Law*. Hideki Kanda eds. *Volume 2: Market Business and Soft Law*. Minoru Nakazato eds. *Volume 3: Government Regulation and Soft Law*. Tetsuya ōbuchi eds. *Volume 4: Intellectual Property and Soft Law*. Akira Kotera eds. *Volume 5: International Society and Soft Law]. [Research in Soft Law*. University of Tokyo Graduate Schools for Law and Politics, 21st Century COE Program. Classes 1–22.]

7　Alexis de Tocqueville"DE LA DEMOCRATIE EN AMERIQUE" 1835, トクビル、松本礼二訳『アメリカのデモクラシー』第1巻（上）（下）、第2巻（上）（下）、2005～2008, 岩波文庫

8　村上春樹『1Q84』2009, 新潮社、**Haruki Murakami**"1Q84" 2013,Vintage;Reprint

9　Tatsuo Inoue"The Poverty of Rights-Blind Communality: Looking Through the Window of Japan"1993,Brigham Young University Law Review, 井上達夫『現代の貧困－リベラリズムの日本社会論』2011, 岩波現代文庫

10　John Owen Haley"Authority Without Power － Law and the Japanese Paradox"1991,Oxford University Press

11　Ulrica Morth"Soft Law in Governance and Regulation-An Interdisciplinary Analysis"2004,Edward Elgar Publishing

12　齋藤純一・田村哲樹編『アクセスデモクラシー論』2012, 日本経済評論社 ,[**Junichi Saito and Tetsuki Tamura** eds.*The Theory of*

Access Democracy]

13　小熊英二『社会を変えるには』2012, 講談社 *[Eiji Oguma,In Order to Change Society]*

14　John Keane"The Life and Death of Democracy"2009、ジョン・キーン森本醇訳『デモクラシー生と死』2013, みすず書房

15　瀬木比呂志『絶望の裁判所』2014, 講談社現代新書 ,*[Hiroshi Segi, The Hopeless of the Courts].*

16　佐藤岩夫・菅原郁夫・山本和彦編『利用者からみた民事訴訟－司法制度改革審議会「民事訴訟利用者調査」の２次分析』2006, 日本評論社 ,*[Iwao Sato, eds. Analysis of Survey in 2000: The User's Opinion as to Civil Litigation.]*

17　黒木亮『法服の王国（上）（下）』2013, 産経新聞出版 ,*[Ryō Kuroki ,The Kingdom of a Judge's Robe (Books 1 and 2).]*

18　神山敏雄『[新版] 日本の経済犯罪－その実状と法的対応』2001, 日本評論社 ,*[Toshio Kamiyama, Economic Crimes in Japan – The Reality and Legal Response]*

19　山岸俊男『社会的ジレンマ「環境破壊」から「いじめ」まで』2011,PHP 研究所 , *[Toshio Yamagishi, Social Dilemmas – from 'Environmental Destruction' to 'Bullying']*

20　Kazumichi Tsutsumi"Market Regulation and Business Crime in the Context of Reciprocity:International, Annals of Criminology"2011, International Society for Criminology,　堤和通『市場の規制とビジネス犯罪－相互性のアイデアからの考察－』警察政策 14 巻 ,2012

21　松原英世『企業活動の刑事規制－抑止機能から意味付与機能へ』2000, 信山社, [Hideyo Matsubara *Criminal Regulation of Company Activities – From a Deterrent Function to Meaningful Function*]

22　John Braithwaite"Restorative Justice and Responsive Regulation"2002,Oxford Univ, John Braithwaite"The World of Restorative Justice", ジョン・ブレイスウェイト 細井陽子訳『修復的司法の世界』2008, 成文堂, John Braithwaite"CORPORATE CRIME in the pharmaceutical Industry"Routledge&Kegan Paul London ,1984, ジョン・ブレイスウェイト 井上眞理子訳『企業犯罪—アメリカ製薬会社における企業犯罪のケース・スタディ』,1992 三一書房

23　川崎友巳『企業の刑事責任』2004, 成文堂, [Tomomi Kawasaki, *The Criminal Responsibility of Companies*]

24　白石賢『企業犯罪・不祥事の法政策－刑事処罰から行政処分・社内処分へ－』2007, 成文堂, [Ken Shiraishi *Legal Policy of Corporate Crimes and Scandals – From Criminal Punishment to Administrative and Corporate Measures*]

25　指宿信『証拠開示と公正な裁判』2012, 現代人文社, [Makoto Ibusuki ,*criminal Discovery and the Fair Trial*]

26　日本法社会学編『特集：裁判員制度の法社会学』法社会学 79 号, 2013, 有斐閣 ,[The Japanese Association of Sociology of Law, *Sociological Jurisprudence of the Lay Judge System*]

27　内田貴『契約の時代－日本社会と契約法』2000, 岩波書店,

[Takashi Uchida ,*The Age of Contracts – Japanese Society and Contract Law*]

28　ROBERT A.KAGAN"Adversarial Legalism-THE AMERICAN WAY OF LAW"2003,HARVARD UNIVERSITY PRESS, ロバート・A・ケイガン　北村喜宣他訳『アメリカ社会の法動態－多元社会アメリカと当事者対抗的リーガリズム』2007,慈学社

29　岡田和樹・齋藤浩『誰が法曹業界をダメにしたのか－もう一度、司法改革を考える－』2013,中公新書ラクレ,[Kazuki Okada and Hiroshi Saito ,*Who Ruined the Business World of Legal Professionals? Reconsidering Judicial Reform*]

30　大沢秀介『現代型訴訟の日米比較』1988,弘文堂, [Hideyuki Oosawa ,*The Modern Form of Litigation – Comparing Japan and America*]

31　Ulrich Beck"Weltrisikogesellschaft,Weltoffentlichkeit und globale Subpolitic"1997,Picus Verlag,Wien , ウルリッヒ・ベック,島村賢一訳『世界リスク社会論　テロ、戦争、自然破壊』2010,ちくま学芸文庫

32　宇賀克也『行政手続法の解説［第5次改訂版］』2005,学陽書房, [Katsuya Uga ,*Commentary on the Administrative Procedure Act (5th Edition)*]

33　原田久『広範囲応答型の官僚制－パブリック・コメント手続の研究－』2011,信山社, [Hisashi Harada,*Broad Scope Response Model of the Bureaucratic System - Research into Public Comment Procedures*]

34　Paul Hirst"Associative Democracy: New Forms of Economic and Social Governance"1994,Polity Press

35　原田大樹『自主規制の公法学的研究』2007,有斐閣 , [Hiroki Harada ,*Public Law Research of Autonomous Regulations*]

36　Luigi Zingales"A Capitalism for the People：Recapturing the Lost Genius of American Prosperity"2012,Basic Books, ルイジ・ジンガレス　若田部昌澄監訳　栗原百代訳『人びとのための資本主義』2013,NTT 出版

37　樋口範雄・土屋裕子編『生命倫理と法』2005,樋口範雄・岩田太編『同Ⅱ』2007,弘文堂 ,[Norio Higuchi, and Yuko Tsuchiya. *Life Ethics and Law*],[Norio Higuchi and Futoshi Iwata. ,*Life Ethics and Law II*]

38　太田勝造『法と正義の相互作用－人間進化における適応の観点から－』法社会学第 78 号　2013,有斐閣 , [Shouzo Ohta, *Reciprocal Function Between Law & Justice.*]

39　松井茂記『日本国憲法　第 2 版』2002,有斐閣 ,[Shigeki Matsui, *Japanese Constitution.*]

40　Michel J.Sandel "Democracy's Discontent: America in Search of a Public Philosophy"1998, マイケル ·J· サンデル , 小林正弥監訳『民主政の不満－公共哲学を求めるアメリカ』2011,勁草書房

41　藤倉徹也『医事事件において医療ガイドラインの果たす役割』2009,判例タイムズ ,[Tetsuya Fujikura,*The Role Played by Medical Guidelines in Medical Cases*]

42　『公益通報制度の体系的立法化に向けての一考察―内部

告発者保護から公益通報制度へ』白石賢, ジュリスト No.1234, 2002,[Ken Shiraishi ,*A Consideration of the Systemic Legislation of the Public Interest Reporting System – From Protecting Whistleblowers to a Public Interest Reporting System*]

43　宇賀克也『情報公開・個人情報保護：最新重要判例・審査会答申の紹介と分析』2013, 有斐閣 ,[Katsuya Uga, *Government Information disclosure・Personal Information Protection: New Important cases.*]

44　阿部泰隆『大震災の法と政策　阪神・淡路大震災に学ぶ政策法学』1996, 日本評論社 ,[Harutaka Abe, *Law & Policy of Great Disaster in Hanshin & Awaji.*]

45　Kiyoshi Kurokawa"Nuclear Safety:Countries'Regulatory Bodies Have Made Changes in Response to the Fukushima Daiichi Accident", 黒川清『国会事故調報告書』2012, 徳間書店

46　山田孝男『小泉純一郎の「原発ゼロ」』2013, 毎日新聞社 , [Takao Yamada ,*Junichirō Koizumi's Zero Reactors*]

47　Lawrence Repeta"Japan's Judicial System Reform Council and Rule of Law", 法社会学 78 号, 2013, 有斐閣

48　藤田友敬『ソフトローの基礎理論』上記注６の第２２号 ,2013,[Tomotaka Fujita ,*The Foundational Theory of Soft Law. supra note 6*]

49　萩原金美『検証・司法制度改革Ⅰ-法科大学院・法曹養成制度を中心に』2013, 中央大学出版部 ,[Kaneyoshi Hagiwara ,*Examination – Reform of the Judicial System I – Law School –*

Focusing on the Education System of Legal Professionals]

50　David S.law "The Anatomy of a Conservative Court:Judicial Review in Japan"2009, David S.law "Why Has Judicial Review Failed in Japan?"2011,David S.law"The Japanese Supreme Court and judical Review"2013、デイヴィッド・S・ロー, 西川伸一訳『日本の最高裁を解剖する－アメリカの研究者からみた日本の司法』2013, 現代人文社

〈引用判例〉　Court Decisions

A 『ハンセン病国家賠償訴訟(熊本地裁平成13年5月11日判決)』医事法判例百選56～59頁
[Lawsuit for State Reparations for Leprosy (Kumamoto District Court 11 May 2001)]

B 『行政処分差止訴訟及び義務不存在確認訴訟の適法性（最高裁平成24年2月9日第一小法廷判決)』平成24年度重要判例解説51～52頁 [Legality of an Administrative Sanctions Injunction Lawsuit and an Absence of Obligation Confirmation Lawsuit (Judgment of the First Petty Bench of the Supreme Court, 9 Feb 2012)]

C 『医薬品のインターネットによる販売規制の適法性（最高裁平成25年1月11日第二小法廷判決)』平成24年度重要判例解説24～25頁 [Legality of the Regulation of Pharmaceutical Sales via the Internet (Judgment of the Second Petty Bench of the

D『宗教上の理由に基づく「剣道」の不受講（最高裁第二小法低平成8年3月8日判決）』憲法判例百選Ⅰ94～95頁 [Abstention from kendo classes based on religious reasons (Judgment of the Second Petty Bench of the Supreme Court, 8 Mar 1996)]

E　東京地裁平成16年（ワ）第10887号損害賠償等請求事件、東京高裁平成19年（ネ）第3357号損害賠償等請求控訴事件、判例秘書ID番号06320287 [Claim for Damages, Case No. Wa-10887, Tokyo District Court 2004; Appeal of Claim for Damages, Case No. Ne-3357, Tokyo District Court 2007]

Fドイツ判例翻訳 (German Judicial Precedent)　http://ameblo.jp/naoya-endo/entry-11521233806.html

G『コンビニ本部の加盟店に対する拘束条件付取引による損害賠償請求が認められた事例（福岡地裁平成23年9月15日判決）』平成23年度重要判例解説269～270頁 [Recognition of Damage Claims for Transactions under Conditions of High Speed by a Convenience Store's Franchises (Kumamoto District Court 15 Sept 2011)]

H『競業避止義務違反の告知による取引妨害、差止請求権の要件の成立－ドライアイス仮処分事件（東京地裁平成23年3月30日決定)』平成23年度重要判例解説271～272頁 [Obstruction of Commerce by Violation of Non-Competition Obligation and the Establishment of Conditions for Injunction Requests – The Dry Ice Temporary Injunction Case (Decision of the Tokyo District Court of 30 Mar 2011)]

I 『本案におけるインカメラ審理の可能性（最高裁平成 21 年 1 月 15 日第一小法廷決定)』平成 21 年度重要判例解説 143 〜 144 頁 [In Favor of the Possibility of In-Camera Trials (Decision of the First Petty Bench of the Supreme Court of 15 Jan 2009)]

〈遠藤直哉出版物〉　Published Works by Naoya Endo

a 「ソフトローによる社会改革」幻冬舎メディアコンサルタント（2012 年）

　　[Social Reform by Soft Law]

b 「ソフトローによる医療改革」幻冬舎メディアコンサルタント（2012 年）

　　[Medical Reform by Soft Law].

c 「新しい法社会を作るのはあなたです－「ソフトロー」と「分割責任論」の活用」アートデイズ（2012 年）

　　[It is You Who Makes a New Legal Society – The Application of 'Soft Law' and 'The Theory of Devided Responsibility']

d 『「ソフトローをめぐる民事機能強化と刑事抑制化の構想－医療・行政・市場・報道における予防規制』小島武司先生古

稀記念論文集「権利実効化のための法政策と司法改革」商事法務 (2009 年)

[Soft Law Surrounding the Scheme for the Strengthening of the Functions of the Civil Justice and Deterrence of Criminal Sanction – Preventative Regulation in Medicine, Administration, the Market, and Broadcasting." Takeshi Kojima's Seventy Years of Age Celebration – Legal Policy and Judicial Reform to Make Rights More Effective.]

e 「ロースクール教育論〜新しい弁護技術と訴訟運営」信山社 (2000 年)

[Law School Education Theory – New Pleading Techniques and Management of Lawsuits].

f 「取締役分割責任論−平成１３年改正商法と株主代表訴訟運営論」信山社 (2002 年)

[The Theory of Devided Responsibility for Directors – Revision to the Commercial Code in 2001 and the Theory of Shareholder Derivative Lawsuits].

g 「危機にある生殖医療への提言〜ジェンダーバラエティー・着床前診断・精子卵子提供・代理出産」近代文芸社 (2004 年)

[An Opinion on Reproductive Medicine in Crisis – Gender Variety, Preimplantation Genetic Diagnosis, Sperm and Egg Donors, Host Mother].

h 「はじまった着床前診断〜流産を繰り返さないための不妊治療」はる書房 (2005 年)（大谷徹郎医師他）

[Initiated Preimplantation Genetic Diagnosis – Infertility Treatment to Prevent Repeated Miscarriages].

i 「いつも野党に投票しよう！－繰り返す政権交代」牧野出版（2008年）

[Let's Always Vote for the Opposition Party! Continuous Change of Government by the party].

j 「生殖補助医療支援基本法の制定の必要性－学術会議（生殖補助医療の在り方検討委員会）への申入書」「法律時報」第80巻1号・日本評論社（2008年）

[The Need to Establish a Reproductive Assisting Medicine Support Law – A Proposal to the Science Council of Japan (Committee on Examining Reproductive Assisting Medicine)".

k 「着床前診断と患者の権利－説明義務違反による治療機会の喪失」, 小野幸二教授古稀記念論文集「21世紀の家族と法」法学書院（2007年）

[Preimplantation Diagnosis and the Rights of the Patient – The Loss of an Opportunity for Treatment because of a Violation of the Obligation to Explain].

l 「居住用財産の配偶者への贈与と詐害行為取消権－諸外国の自宅保護制度政策と日本の遅れている現状」(村谷晃司・高柳孔明) 小野幸二教授古稀記念論文集「21世紀の家族と法」法学書院（2007年）

[Donations to One's Spouse of Shared Property and the Right of Recession for Fraudulent Injury – The Policy of Home

Protection in Various Countries, and the Situation in Japan Ibid]. [Family and Law in the 21st Century]". Compilation of Essays for Kōji Ono's Seventy Years of Age Celebration

m 「《座談会》実定法諸分野における実務と学説」「法律時報」第 79 巻 1 号・日本評論社（2007 年）

[Round Table Discussion – Practice and Theory in Various Areas of Positive Law]."

n 「全検証ピンクチラシ裁判」一葉社（1993 年）（清水英夫編著）

[A Complete Examination of the Trial on Flyers Advertising Sex-Related Businesses].

o 「中立型調整弁護士モデルの展望」変革の中の弁護士・下巻、有斐閣（1993 年）

[Lawyers in Reform: Second Volume – Development of the Neutral-Style Regulative Lawyer Model].

p 「労災職業病の企業責任－アスベスト」労災職業病健康管理Ⅰ 総合労働研究所（1984 年・1992 年）

[Corporate Responsibility for Occupational Diseases – Asbestos].

q 「アスベスト対策をどうするか」日本評論社（1988 年）鈴木武夫・田尻宗昭編著

[What to Do About Asbestos Countermeasures?].

r 「民事訴訟促進と証拠収集」判例タイムズ 665 号（1988 年）

[Promotion of Civil Litigation and Evidence Collection]

〈遠藤直哉経歴〉 Background of Naoya Endo

1945年生まれ。フェアネス法律事務所代表弁護士。法学博士(中央大学)。米国法社会学会会員。

麻布高校卒。東京大学法学部卒。ワシントン大学ロースクール大学院修士。第二東京弁護士会平成8年度副会長。法曹養成二弁センター委員長。桐蔭横浜法科大学院教授歴任。

Fairness Law Firm Representative Attorney. Doctor of Laws (Chuo University). Member of Low and Society Association.

Born in 1945. Graduated from Azabu High School, University of Tokyo Faculty of Law, University of Washington School of Law (L.L.M). Vice Chairman of 2nd Tokyo Bar Association in 1996. Chairman of the 2nd Tokyo Bar Association Legal Training Center. Professor at Toin Yokohama University Law School in various posts.

ソフトロー・デモクラシーによる法改革
THE REFORM OF JAPANESE LAW
　　　VIA SOFT LAW DEMOCRACY

2014年5月10日　初版第1刷発行

著　　者　遠藤直哉
Author　Noya Endo
装　　丁　横山　恵
発 行 者　宮島正洋
発 行 所　株式会社アートデイズ
Published 2014 by Art Days Inc.
　　　　　〒160-0008 東京都新宿区三栄町 17 Ｖ四谷ビル
　　　　　電話 03-3353-2298　FAX 03-3353-5887
　　　　　http://www.artdays.co.jp
印 刷 所　倉敷印刷株式会社
　　　　　　　　　　　　乱丁・落丁本はお取替えいたします。

全国書店にて好評発売中!!

新しい法社会を作るのはあなたです
——「ソフトロー」と「分割責任論」の活用——

法学博士・弁護士 **遠藤直哉** 著

悪法は守らなくてよい!

法に対する考え方を変えなければ、日本人は幸せになれない。ポスト原発も見据え、新しい法社会づくりには「ソフトロー」と「分割責任論」とが欠かせない。

目次から

法律を守っていれば幸せになれるか？／悪法まで守るべきか／福島原発事故について／司法・検察・警察・自衛隊の改革／医療・経済・政治の改革／法とは何か／ソフトローはどのように積極活用すればいいのか／正しく法を扱うこと／良い法社会を作っていくために、5つの「すぐにできること」／分割責任論の類型／裁判実務の中の分割責任

本体1300円＋税　発行 アートデイズ